Questions & Answers BOOK of FACTS

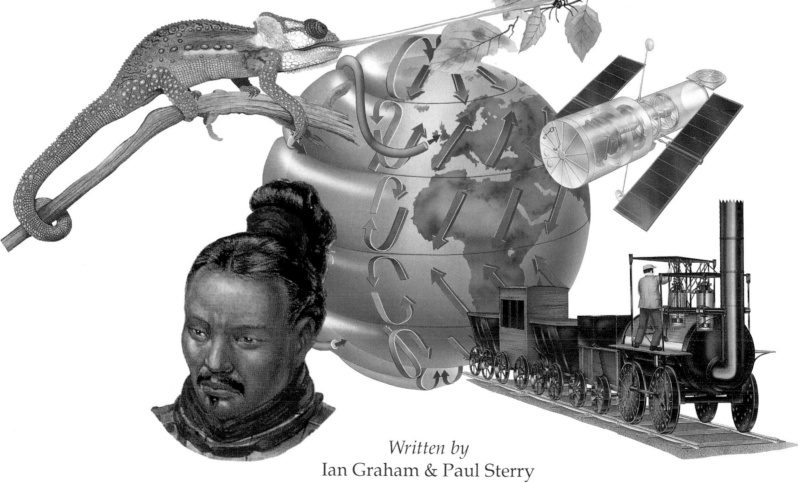

Written by
Ian Graham & Paul Sterry

Vineyard
BOOKS

Specially prepared for
Chapters
90 Ronson Drive
Etobicoke
Ontario M9W 1C1

Planned and produced by
Andromeda Oxford Limited
11–15 The Vineyard
Abingdon
Oxon OX14 3PX

ISBN 1-871869-98-6

Printed in Singapore

CONTENTS

STARS & GALAXIES

Q What is a constellation?

A A constellation is a group of stars. Ancient astronomers gave many of them names, because they thought their patterns in the night sky made shapes that reminded them of things such as animals and gods. Many constellations are visible on a clear night. Some of these are shown below. There are 88 constellations.

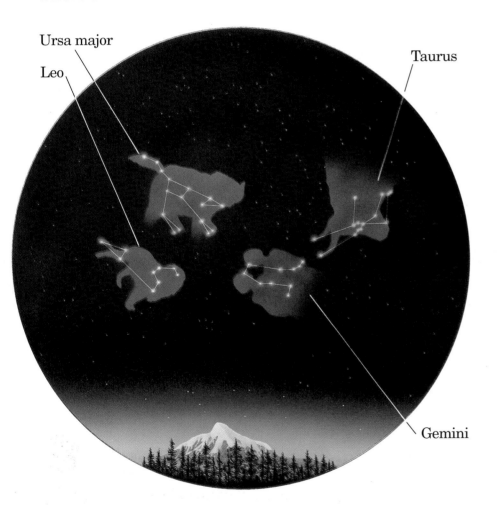

Ursa major

Leo

Taurus

Gemini

Q What is a solar eclipse?

A As the Earth orbits the Sun, and the Moon orbits the Earth, all three sometimes line up. A solar eclipse (above) occurs when the Moon passes in front of the Sun and blocks out its light.

Q What shape is the Milky Way?

A The Sun is one of 100 billion stars that form a galaxy called the Milky Way. If we could look at the Milky Way from the outside, it would look like a glowing ball surrounded by a thin disk of curling arms. We live in one of the galaxy's arms. Because of its shape, the Milky Way is called a spiral galaxy.

Q How was our Solar System formed?

A About 4.6 billion years ago, a cloud of gas and dust began to spiral inward on itself (1). The center of the cloud heated up (2) and matter streamed out from its poles (3). The spinning cloud flattened into a disk (4). The hot core became the Sun. The planets formed from clumps of matter in the disk (5).

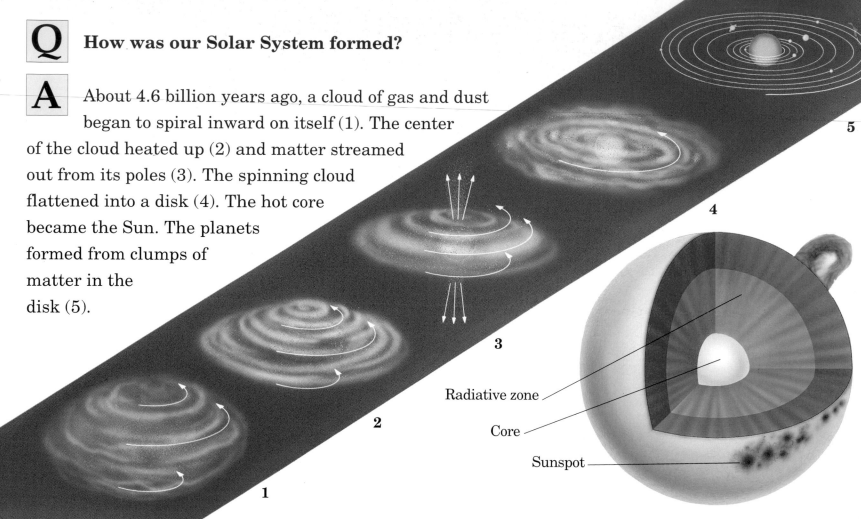

Radiative zone

Core

Sunspot

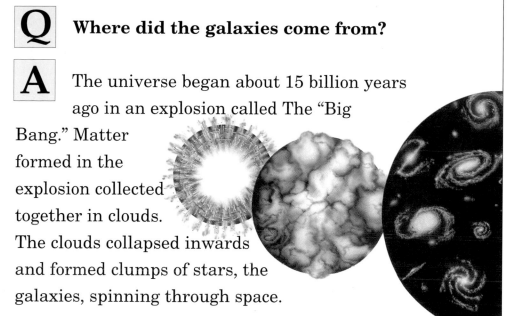

Q Where did the galaxies come from?

A The universe began about 15 billion years ago in an explosion called The "Big Bang." Matter formed in the explosion collected together in clouds. The clouds collapsed inwards and formed clumps of stars, the galaxies, spinning through space.

Q What is a star?

A A star, like the Sun (above), is a large, burning ball of gases. The gas is mostly hydrogen. The hydrogen atoms are packed so tightly in the star's core that they join together to make a different gas, helium. This process, called nuclear fusion, releases an enormous amount of energy, which produces heat and light.

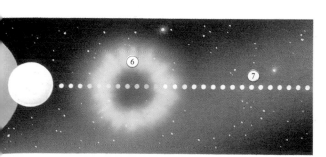

Q How does a star die?

A When a star like the Sun (left) burns all of its hydrogen, it begins to die. It puffs up to form a star called a red giant. It then shrinks and cools to become a tiny white dwarf star.

THE PLANETS

Q What are planets made of?

A The planets that are closest to the Sun, from
Mercury to Mars, are small, rocky worlds. They
have a metal center, or core, surrounded by a thick
mantle of rock with a thin, rocky crust on the surface.
The outer planets are very different. Jupiter and Saturn
are made mostly of hydrogen. Uranus and Neptune
have a rocky core surrounded
by ice and hydrogen (below).
Pluto is made of rock,
with an icy coating.

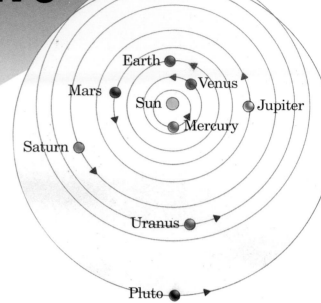

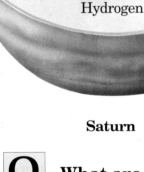

Core

Hydrogen

Saturn

Core

Hydrogen and ice

Uranus

Q How do the planets orbit
the Sun?

A All the planets in the Solar
System travel in the same
direction around the Sun (above). Their
paths are slightly flattened circles called
ellipses. Pluto's orbit is pushed so much
to one side that it crosses Neptune's orbit.

Q What are planets?

A Planets are worlds that
orbit the Sun. The
word "planet" comes from a
Greek word meaning
wanderer, because of the
strange wandering paths they
appear to have when seen
from Earth. There are nine
planets (right). Mercury is the
closest to the Sun, then Venus,
Earth, Mars, Jupiter, Saturn,
Uranus, Neptune and Pluto.

Mercury   Venus   Earth   Mars   Jupiter

Q What is the Great Red Spot?

A Jupiter's Great Red Spot (below) is a swirling storm 18,600 miles across. It was first seen by astronomers as long ago as 1664. Storms on Earth last a few weeks at most. The Great Red Spot has lasted for centuries because Jupiter has no solid surface to slow it down.

Great Red Spot

Q Which planets have moons?

A Only Mercury and Venus do not have moons. Earth has one moon. Mars has two (above). Jupiter has 16 moons. One of them, Ganymede, is larger than the planet Mercury. Saturn has 19 moons, Uranus 15, Neptune eight while Pluto has only one.

Q Is there life on other planets?

A Most of the planets are too harsh to support life as we know it. For many years, people thought that there might be life on Mars. Some astronomers thought they saw lines and dark patches on the planet that might be canals carrying water to grow plants. But when two Viking spacecraft landed there in 1976 and tested the soil, they found no signs of life.

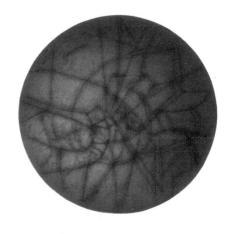

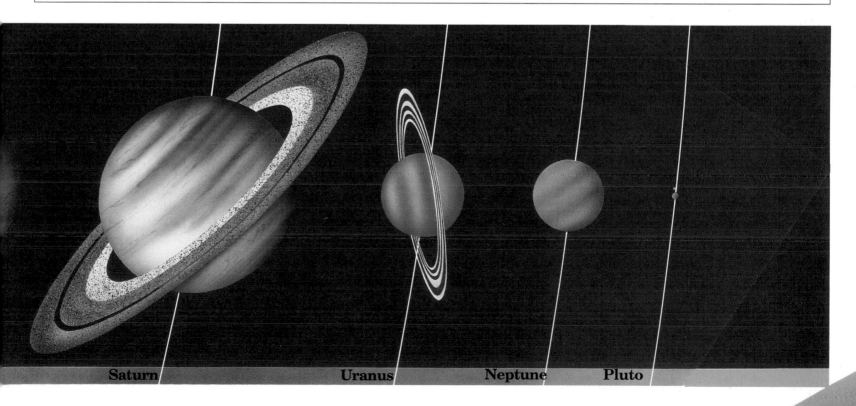

Saturn   Uranus   Neptune   Pluto

Q How did early astronomers study the heavens?

A Astronomers studied the sky with the naked eye until the 17th century. In 1609 the Italian astronomer Galileo Galilei (above) became the first person to study the sky with a telescope.

Q What did Giotto tell us about comets?

A In 1986, the Giotto space probe (below) studied Halley's Comet. A comet consists of a lump of rock and ice called the nucleus, inside a cloud of gas and dust called the coma (inset). It also has a bright tail. Giotto's photographs show a nucleus measuring 5 miles by 7.4 miles. Its instruments found that the coma and tail are made of dust and water vapor.

Q How does a modern telescope work?

A There are two types of telescope. A refractor uses a lens to form an image. A reflector uses a curved mirror. Most modern telescopes used in astronomy are reflectors. The telescope is finely balanced and turns slowly to keep the image steady as the Earth moves. A Schmidt telescope (right) is used to photograph large areas of the sky.

Schmidt telescope gathering light from the stars

Counterbalance

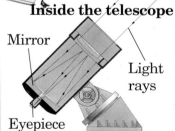

Inside the telescope

Mirror

Light rays

Eyepiece

Q Why is the Hubble telescope in space?

A Light from distant stars passes through the Earth's atmosphere before it reaches a telescope on the ground. The swirling atmosphere makes the stars twinkle. Modern telescopes are usually built on top of mountains, where the atmosphere is thinner, to reduce this effect. The Hubble Space Telescope (below) can see more clearly than any telescope on Earth because it is above the atmosphere.

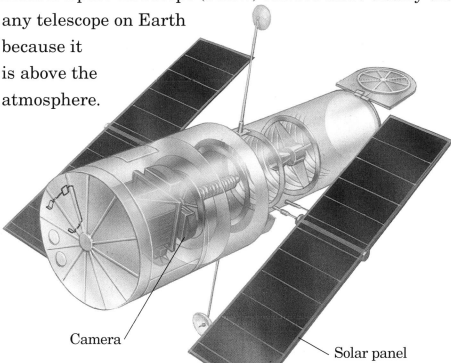

Camera

Solar panel

Q How did the Pioneer space probes work?

A Pioneer 10 and 11 were the first spacecraft to visit the outer Solar System. They were designed to find out if a spacecraft could travel through the asteroid belt, a swarm of rocks orbiting the Sun between Mars and Jupiter. Most spacecraft use solar cells to make electricity from sunlight. Pioneer 10 and 11 traveled so far from the Sun that solar cells would not work. Instead, they carried nuclear power generators to make electricity.

Q Where did the Voyager space probes go?

A Voyager 1 and 2 were launched in 1977. The pull of gravity from the outer planets guided the spacecraft from one planet to the next. Voyager 1 flew past Jupiter in 1979 (below) and Saturn in 1980. Voyager 2 flew past Jupiter (1979), Saturn (1981), Uranus (1986) and Neptune (1989). Their cameras and instruments studied each planet. All the information was sent back to Earth by radio.

Pioneer 11

Thruster

Cosmic ray telescope

Nuclear power generator

SPACE

9

MAN IN SPACE

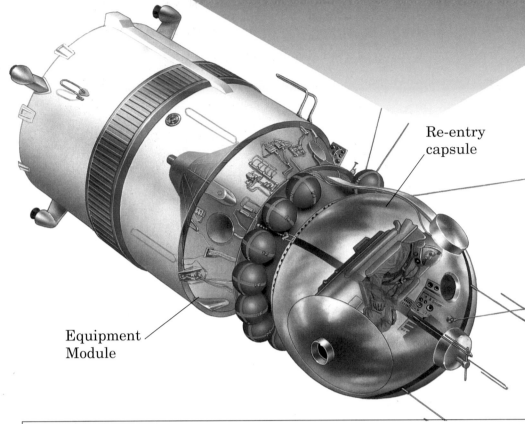

Re-entry capsule

Equipment Module

A The first man in space was Yuri Gagarin from the former Soviet Union. On April 12, 1961, his tiny Vostok space capsule (left), only 2.3 metres across, made one orbit of the Earth. The spherical capsule then separated from its Equipment Module and rocket before plunging back into the Earth's atmosphere and landing by parachute.

Q How did astronauts land on the Moon?

A Apollo astronauts traveled to the Moon in a spacecraft made from three modules linked together. They lived in the cone-shaped Command Module. A Service Module supplied it with oxygen and electric power. Once they were in orbit around the Moon, two of the three astronauts moved into the Lunar Module. They separated it from the rest of the spacecraft and landed on the Moon.

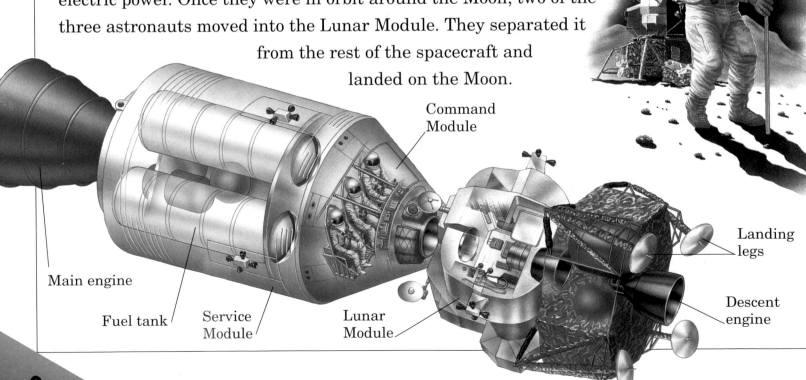

Command Module

Landing legs

Descent engine

Main engine

Fuel tank

Service Module

Lunar Module

Q How do cosmonauts return to Earth?

A Before the Space Shuttle, all American manned spacecraft landed in the Pacific Ocean. Russian Soyuz spacecraft (below) are brought down on land. The small Re-entry Module descends through the atmosphere by parachute. Just before it touches the ground, rockets in the base of the spacecraft fire to cushion the landing.

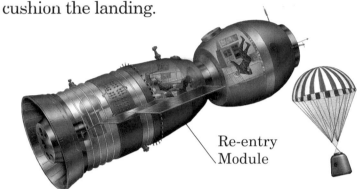

Re-entry Module

Q How is a space station built?

A A space station is far too big to launch in one piece. Instead, it is launched in sections that have to be connected together in space. The Russian space station Mir (right) was launched in four pieces. The base unit was launched first in 1986. It was followed by three more modules that were linked to the base unit.

Solar panel

Base unit

Control center

Soyuz crew ferry

Docking port

Q How does the Space Shuttle take off?

A Six seconds before lift-off, three rocket engines in the Space Shuttle's tail fire. They burn fuel supplied by the huge fuel tank underneath the spacecraft (below). Then the rocket boosters on each side of the fuel tank fire. Clamps holding the spacecraft down on the launch-pad are released and the Space Shuttle takes off.

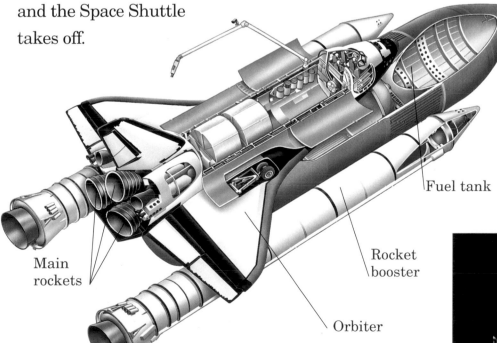

Fuel tank

Main rockets

Rocket booster

Orbiter

Q What will spacecraft look like in the future?

A Future spacecraft will probably be powered by new types of engines instead of rockets. The ramscoop (below) collects hydrogen atoms from space in a large funnel and its engine fuses them together to release energy. The photon sail (bottom) is "blown" through space by light from the Sun or lasers.

SPACE

Q What is beneath
the Earth's surface?

A The Earth's inner core (below) is a solid ball
about 1,500 miles across made of iron and
nickel. This is surrounded by an
outer core about 1,400 miles
thick made of molten iron
and nickel. Outside this
lies the mantle, made
from rock about 1,900
miles thick. The
outside layer is a thin
rocky crust up to 50
miles thick.

Q What are volcanoes?

A Volcanoes are holes in the Earth's crust
which allow molten rock to escape from
beneath. The molten rock, or lava, may flow out
gently or it may be blasted high in the air with
gas and ash in a violent explosion. When
volcanic eruptions pile up the lava into a cone-
shaped mountain
(below), this is also
called a volcano.

— Lava

Volcanic cone

Q Is the seabed flat?

A Underneath the world's oceans
(above), the seabed is divided by
mountain ridges up to 2.5 miles high,
2,500 miles wide and 25,000 miles long.
Molten rock constantly erupts at the
ridges, forming a new seabed which
spreads out on each side.

Q What is a rift valley?

A When magma, or lava, wells up
underground, it pushes up the
crust above it, stretching and cracking
the surface. The cracked crust sinks
and forms a valley with steep sides and
a flat bottom, called a rift valley. The
valley may flood with water to form a
new ocean.

Q Why do rivers flow?

A Rivers flow because water runs downhill. Mountain streams fed by rain or melting snow meet and form a river (below). Streams that flow into rivers are called tributaries. Further down, where the slope is gentler, the river is slower and wider. Finally, it flows out into the sea.

Q What is continental drift?

A Continental drift is the movement of Earth's land masses. There was once a single continent which we call Pangaea. The rest of the Earth was covered with water. About 200 million years ago, Pangaea split up. The pieces slowly drifted apart and became today's continents (above).

Q Where are the world's highest mountains?

A Mountains are formed by movements of the Earth's crust. The edges of continents are pushed and squeezed together, thrusting up the land in the process. The highest mountain range is the Himalayas (below). Its highest peak is Mount Everest (29,028 feet above sea level).

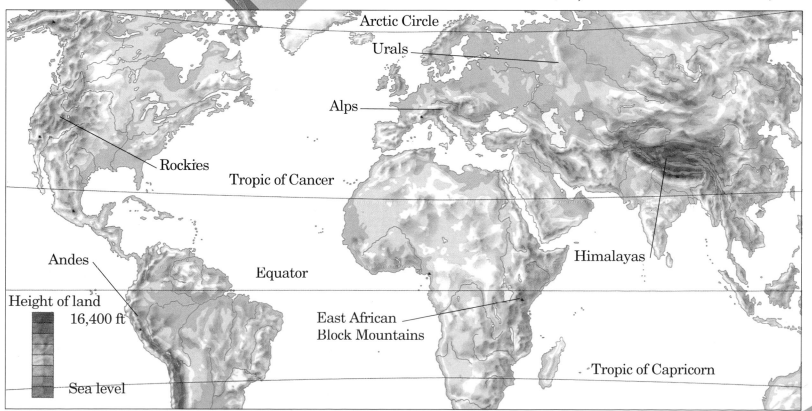

Arctic Circle

Urals

Alps

Rockies

Tropic of Cancer

Andes

Equator

Height of land
16,400 ft

East African
Block Mountains

Himalayas

Tropic of Capricorn

Sea level

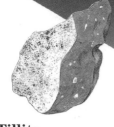

Tillite

Marble

Syenite

Q What are the main types of rocks?

A There are three main types of rock – igneous, sedimentary and metamorphic (above). Igneous rock such as syenite is solidified lava. Sedimentary rock such as tillite is formed from compressed particles. Metamorphic rock such as marble is made from rock changed by heat or pressure.

Q How do we obtain rocks and minerals?

A Rocks and minerals are taken out of the ground by mining (below). If they are near the surface, they can be mined by scraping the earth away. This is open cast or strip mining. Deeper minerals are mined by shaft mining. Deep shafts are dug and miners tunnel out from the shafts to extract the minerals.

Q What is a mineral?

A Rocks are made from minerals. Each mineral is made from a different set of chemicals. Most rocks contain several minerals. Olivine is a green mineral found in basalt. Quartz is the most common mineral on Earth. Galena contains lead.

Olivine

Galena

Quartz

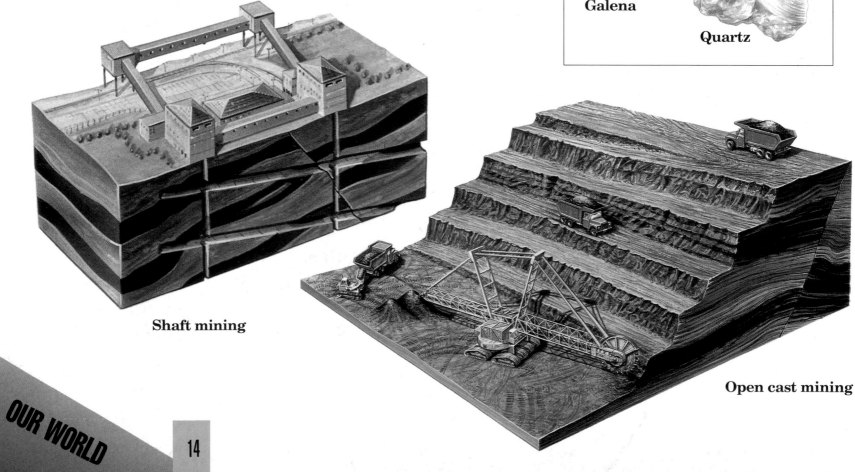

Shaft mining

Open cast mining

Q How did ancient people use stone?

A People have used stone for making things since prehistoric times. The first humans made axes and knives from flint. The Egyptians built stone pyramids to house the bodies of their kings. The Ancient Greeks built temples to their gods. The roofs were supported by massive stone columns. The Romans carved stone statues of their gods and leaders (right).

Pyramid building

Greek column

Roman statue

Q What are fossils?

A Fossils are the remains of prehistoric animals and plants preserved in rock. When an animal or plant died, it sometimes sank into soil or mud. The animal or plant rotted away and its shape was replaced by minerals.

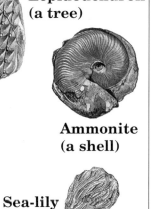

Lepidodendron (a tree)

Ammonite (a shell)

Sea-lily

Q What are gems?

A Gems are rare and beautiful stones found in the Earth's crust. Most are crystals made of minerals. Opal and amethyst are two forms of silica. Sapphire is made of corundum. Diamond is made from a single element – carbon. Gems are cut to size, polished and made into jewelry with gold or silver (below).

Diamond

Diamond ring

Q How are rocks changed by heat?

A When hot, molten magma forces its way up through the Earth's crust (below), it changes the surrounding rocks. For example, limestone, which is soft and crumbly, becomes harder and changes into marble. The rising magma is called an igneous intrusion.

Opal

Sapphire

Amethyst

Igneous intrusion

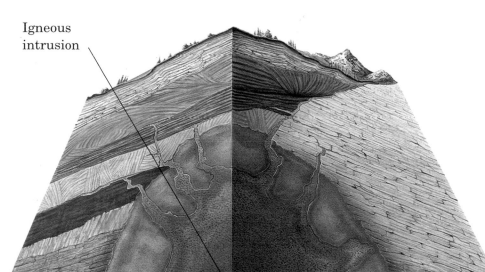

OUR WORLD

Q What causes the winds?

A Winds are created because of differences in air temperature and air pressure. When air is heated at the Equator (below), it rises, cools and then sinks over the tropics. Some moves back again towards the equator, creating the trade winds. The rest is drawn towards the poles as westerly winds.

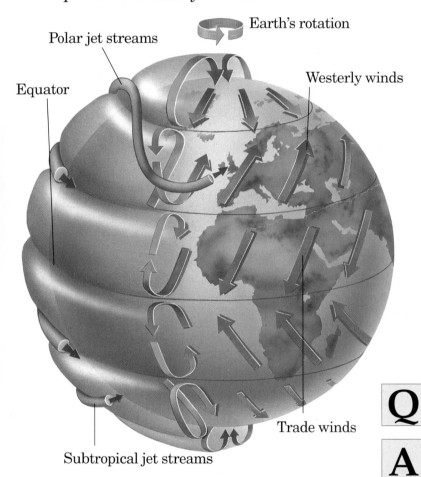

Earth's rotation

Polar jet streams

Westerly winds

Equator

Trade winds

Subtropical jet streams

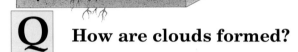

Water vapor in clouds

Water falls as rain

Q How are clouds formed?

A Water evaporates from land, lakes and sea (above) and is carried by the air as water vapor. Warm air can hold more water vapor than cold air. As warm air rises and cools, for example over a mountain, the water vapor condenses to water, forming clouds. Eventually, the water falls from the clouds as rain. The rainwater runs back into the rivers and lakes.

Q What is erosion?

A Erosion is the breaking down of solid rock into smaller particles which are then carried away. Wind, water, gravity, sea and rain are common natural causes of erosion and so is ice (below). The frozen ice in the glacier carves U-shaped valleys as it moves slowly downhill. Most mountain valleys are formed in this way. Today, human activity also causes damaging erosion.

Ice

Water

Gravity

Wind

Sea

Q What is energy conservation?

A We use a lot of energy in our homes. Much of it comes from oil, coal or gas, which are fossil fuels that will one day be used up. If we insulate our houses better, and trap the Sun's heat, we use less fuel. This is called energy conservation. We can also use ever-lasting energy sources, such as wind (below).

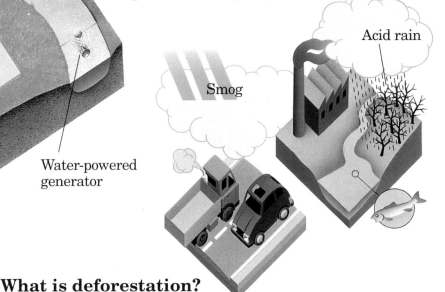

Wind-powered generator

Solar panel

Heat insulation

Water-powered generator

Methane generator

Q Why is pollution harmful?

A Many of the fumes and chemicals produced by cars or industry (below) can damage plants and animals. Even small amounts of some polluting gases or liquids can kill large numbers of living things and many are also poisonous to people as well.

Acid rain

Smog

Q What is deforestation?

A Forests once covered about 15 billion acres of the Earth but now only 10 billion acres are left (below). The process of cutting down trees is called deforestation, and is carried out by people. Trees are important to our survival because, like other green plants, they produce oxygen. Without oxygen, animals cannot survive.

Q How does the peppered moth adapt to pollution?

A The peppered moth rests on tree bark where its camouflage hides it from bird predators. The bark in polluted towns may be black and normal camouflage would be useless. In these areas, a black-winged form of the moth is found.

Normal form   **Black-winged form**

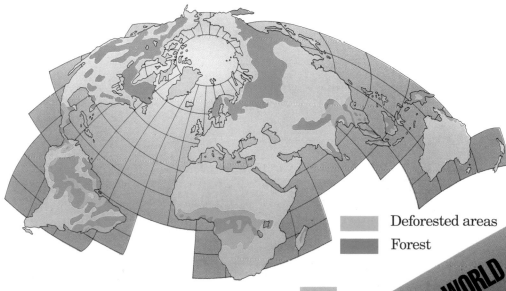

Deforested areas

Forest

HABITATS

Q What lives in a habitat?

A A habitat is a particular place, such as a woodland or a pond. Certain plants and animals are suited to living there, and nowhere else. They have adapted to living in that habitat. In this pond scene (below), the fish and plants can only live in the water, not on dry land. Birds such as herons and swans only feed and nest in watery habitats.

Q What is an endangered species?

A An endangered species is one which is rare and threatened with extinction. The manatee has become rare because of hunting and pollution. The koala is threatened by drought and fire, while the kakapo, a New Zealand parrot, has been hunted, and is now killed by rats and cats.

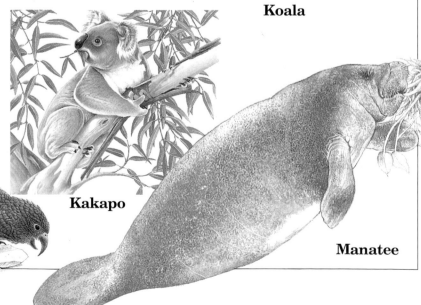

Koala

Kakapo

Manatee

Q How do habitats change?

A Although people alter habitats, the process also happens naturally. This cross-section through a pond (right) shows the gradual process of filling-in. Over the years, the roots of the water plants trap silt, so the pond holds less and less water. The pond becomes silted up and will eventually become dry land.

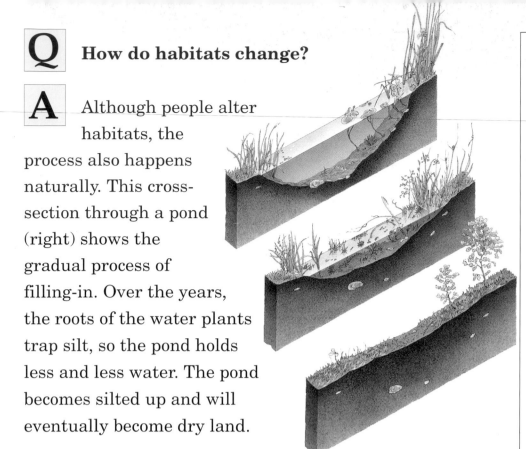

Q What is a food web?

A A food web (below) is a way of showing how plants and animals in a habitat depend on each other. The arrows show which species provide food for other species. Some of the small animals are food for a number of larger predators.

Q How do animals adapt to changes in their environment?

A In many parts of the world the environment changes with the seasons. When winter comes, some animals hibernate while others migrate. The arctic hare has adapted to winter snowfall by molting its brown summer coat for a white winter one. This gives it camouflage throughout the year.

Q What is a microhabitat?

A Every habitat contains lots of smaller habitats called microhabitats. The creatures that live there are specially adapted to its conditions. These mites, for example, can only survive among particles of soil.

COUNTRIES & PEOPLE

Q Which continent has most countries?

A The continent with the most countries is Africa. There are 53 independent countries in Africa. The largest African country is Sudan. It has an area of 966,751 square miles. The African country with the most people is Nigeria, with a population of over 100 million.

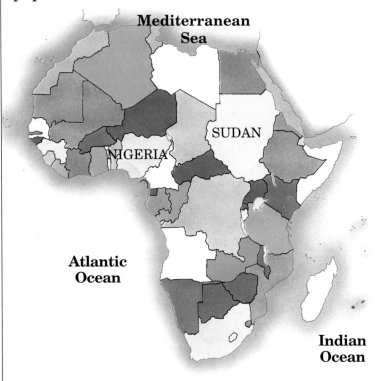

Mediterranean Sea

SUDAN

NIGERIA

Atlantic Ocean

Indian Ocean

Q Why do countries have flags?

A Every country has its own flag. Flags are used as a way of identifying the country, or anything belonging to it, to other nations. The flags above belong to countries that are members of the United Nations.

Q How many people are there in the world?

A More than 5.5 billion people live on the Earth. By the end of the 20th century the population will have reached 6.5 billion. Some places, such as deserts and polar regions, are largely unsuitable for people. Most people live where there is rich farmland or where cities can provide jobs and housing (below). The most populated country is China; it has over a billion people.

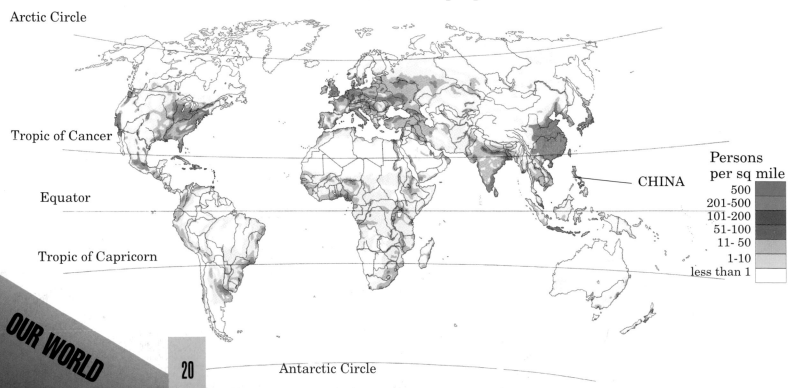

Arctic Circle

Tropic of Cancer

Equator

Tropic of Capricorn

CHINA

Persons per sq mile
500
201-500
101-200
51-100
11- 50
1-10
less than 1

Antarctic Circle

A Over many thousands of years, people in different parts of the world have developed variations in appearance and hair or skin color. People of similar appearance and color are said to belong to the same race. There are three main races: Negroid, Caucasoid and Mongoloid (below). Their world distribution is shown on the map.

Mongoloid
Negroid
Caucasoid

A Festivals celebrate special days such as a time of year, like the Chinese New Year (below), or an important event such as the founding of a country, like Australia Day (right).

Q Why do people wear a national costume?

A Modern dress is similar in many parts of the world, so many people remember their heritage by wearing a national costume on festival days. The costume usually has a long history. The Breton people of northwest France have a very distinctive costume (right).

21

OUR WORLD

EVOLUTION

Q What is evolution?

A The first forms of life appeared on Earth many hundreds of millions of years ago. They were tiny, primitive creatures that lived in water. As millions of years went by, these creatures gradually changed and many different forms of life slowly appeared (above). This process is called evolution and it is still continuing today.

Q What does extinction mean?

A Extinction occurs when the last individual of a plant or animal species dies out. In the past, many creatures such as dinosaurs died out naturally – perhaps because of changes in the climate. In the last few centuries, animals such as the dodo (left) and the Tasmanian wolf (below) have been hunted to extinction by people.

Q How do we know about the past?

A We find out about the past from fossils. If a prehistoric animal died in shallow, muddy water, its body might become covered with layers of silt which eventually formed solid rock. The soft parts decayed but the skeleton slowly absorbed minerals and hardened in the rock to become a fossil (left). Millions of years later, if the rock is worn away, we can find the fossils.

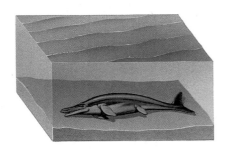

Q What is natural selection?

A Not all animals are as strong as others of the same species. This deer was not fast enough to escape a tiger attack and it will be killed. Other, fitter deer will evade capture and survive to breed. This process of survival of the fittest is called natural selection.

Q How did the horse evolve?

A The horse evolved from a rabbit-sized animal called *Hyracotherium* that lived 50 million years ago. Its descendants such as *Mesohippus* and *Merychippus* grew larger and became grazing animals. The number of toes in the foot dwindled from four to one, which improved its running speed, and eventually the modern horse (below) evolved.

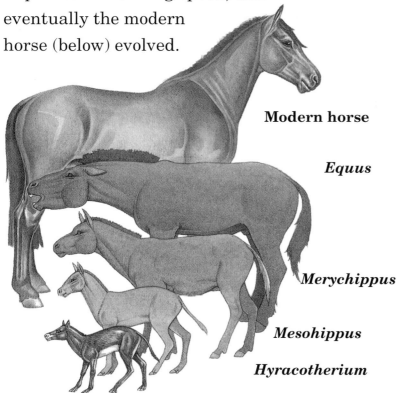

Modern horse

Equus

Merychippus

Mesohippus

Hyracotherium

Q What is adaptation?

A Animals and plants often develop traits that help them survive. Such traits are called adaptations. This tree-living tarsier is adapted with long legs for leaping, sucker-like clinging toes and large eyes for seeing at night.

Q When did our ancestors evolve?

A Our first true ancestor was the ape-like *Ramapithecus* (right). It lived about 8 million years ago, mainly in trees, but also foraged on the ground for food. Fossil bones have been found in Africa, Europe and India. *Australopithecus*, the next link in the chain, lived some 3 million years ago in East Africa.

Q What were the first animals like?

A The first animals were probably single-celled creatures. Their bodies had no hard parts so they did not form fossils. The first animals that we know from fossils lived 570 million years ago. Many had worm-like or plant-like bodies. Others had armored head shields (below).

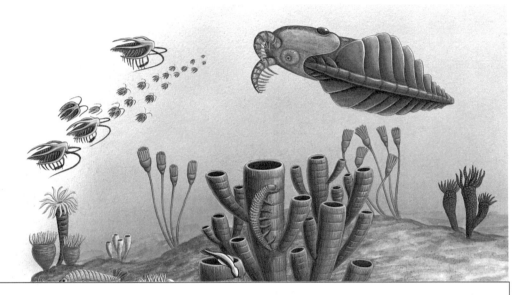

Q How did *Pterodactylus* fly?

A *Pterodactylus* (above) had a lightweight, furry body and was able to fly using its long, membranous wings. These were attached to the wrist bones and the bones of the fourth finger. *Pterodactylus* probably clung to cliff edges and then launched itself into the air, where it glided over the sea snatching fish from the surface.

Q What did prehistoric fish eat?

A Although no one can be completely sure, the diet of prehistoric fish probably consisted of worm-like creatures and mollusks. Some of the larger species of fish had numerous sharp teeth. They might have chased and eaten other fish, in a similar way to modern-day sharks and barracuda.

Cryptoclidus

Ichthyosaurus

Peloneustes

Q **Which reptiles ruled the seas?**

A In ancient times, the seas were ruled by ichthyosaurs and plesiosaurs (above). Both had streamlined bodies and paddle-shaped limbs. *Ichthyosaurus* resembled a cross between a fish and a dolphin. Some plesiosaurs, such as *Cryptoclidus,* had long necks; others, like *Peloneustes*, were whale-like. Ichthyosaurs and plesiosaurs ate mainly fish, but some plesiosaurs also ate one another.

Q **How did mammals survive the Ice Age?**

A As the Ice Age approached and the climate became colder, many mammals grew larger. This is because large animals retain their body heat better than small ones. Heat retention was also helped by growing thick, furry coats, such as that seen in the woolly mammoth (left). Thick layers of fat beneath the skin provided insulation. Other large, hairy mammals that survived the Ice Age included woolly rhinoceroses and giant cave bears.

Q **What were the terror cranes?**

A Terror cranes were giant birds that lived some 50 million years ago in North America. They stood 6.6 feet tall and hunted small mammals in areas of open grassland. They had strong legs for running and a powerful, hook-tipped bill for dealing with their prey. Terror cranes are given the scientific name *Diatryma*.

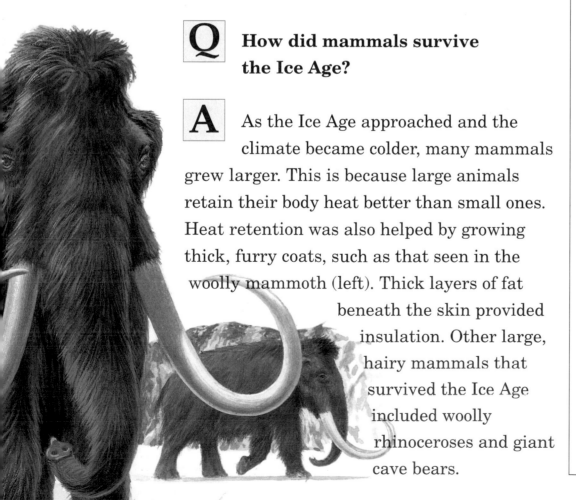

NATURE

DINOSAURS

Triceratops

Leptoceratops

 Q Which was the tallest dinosaur?

A Many of the huge, plant-eating dinosaurs had long necks. The tallest was *Brachiosaurus* (above) which not only had a long neck but long front legs as well. It could stretch up to 40 feet and probably fed on the tops of trees, much as giraffes do today. It needed legs the size of tree trunks to support its great weight.

Q Why did some dinosaurs have armoured heads?

A Some dinosaurs were meat-eating predators. Not surprisingly, many of the plant-eating dinosaurs developed armored heads to help defend themselves (above). The head of *Triceratops* was covered with a large plate and carried three, forward-pointing horns. *Leptoceratops* was much smaller and lacked *Triceratops*' horns.

 Q Which was the most fearsome meat-eater?

A *Tyrannosaurus* (right) was probably the most terrifying carnivorous dinosaur. It was certainly one of the largest. The head was huge and its skull was larger than a man. *Tyrannosaurus* stood upright on massive hind legs and could outrun slower, plant-eating dinosaurs. Its teeth, which were 6 inches long, were used to rip and tear the flesh of its prey.

Tyrannosaurus skull

Q How did *Stegosaurus* get warm?

A *Stegosaurus* was a large, 25-foot-long dinosaur with a double row of armored plates on its back. These may have been useful in defense but were probably also used to control body temperature. They would have gathered heat from the Sun's rays to warm *Stegosaurus* up. Breezes passing through the plates would have helped *Stegosaurus* cool off if it was too hot.

Q Were all dinosaurs big?

A Although some dinosaurs were the largest land animals ever to have lived, many were tiny. Among the smallest were species of *Compsognathus* (left). Some were the size of a chicken. Most *Compsognathus* species had long legs and were good runners. This one is trying to catch a dragonfly.

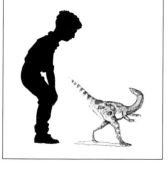

Q How do we know what dinosaurs looked like?

A We can tell what dinosaurs looked like from fossils. These are found in sedimentary rocks from all over the world. Often just a few dinosaur bones are found but sometimes scientists discover a complete skeleton.

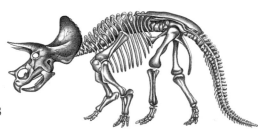

NATURE

SIMPLE CREATURES

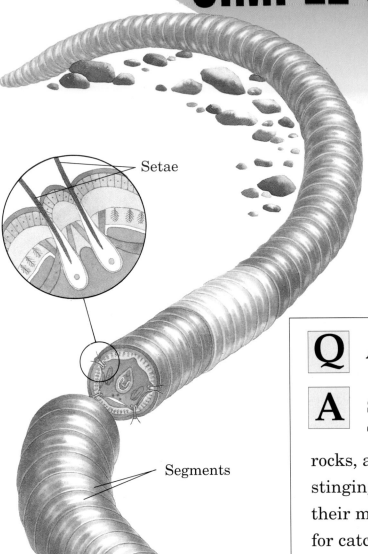

Setae

Segments

Mouth

Q What is inside an earthworm?

A An earthworm's body (left) is made up of compartments called segments. The intestine and the nervous system run the entire length of the body. The hearts, brain and reproductive organs are found near the front of the body. Each segment carries bristly hairs called setae. These help the worm grip the ground when moving.

Q Are sea anemones plants or animals?

A Sea anemones are simple marine animals. They live attached to rocks, and have a ring of stinging tentacles around their mouth which they use for catching food. Some sea anemones can pull the tentacles inside (right).

Q What is a protozoan?

A Protozoa are tiny animals made from a single cell. Although small, these cells are very complex and enable the animal to feed, breathe, excrete and reproduce. Protozoa are very common in soil and water. Some have a rigid shape while others have no fixed shape at all.

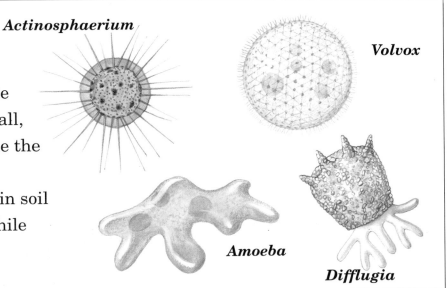

Actinosphaerium

Volvox

Amoeba

Difflugia

Q How does a Portuguese man-of-war swim?

A The Portuguese man-of-war (left) is a large, poisonous, jellyfish-like creature with tentacles up to 59 feet long. It lives in the ocean but does not actually swim. It has a float filled with air which keeps it on the surface, and a sail which carries the animal on the breeze.

Q Why do crabs walk sideways?

A Crabs have their walking legs placed beneath their bodies. If it were to walk forwards or backwards, the crab would trip over its own legs. Instead, crabs scuttle sideways over the seabed so their legs do not touch.

Q How does the cleaner shrimp get its name?

A The cleaner shrimp (below) removes parasites from fish such as this butterfly fish. Both animals benefit. The shrimp gets a tasty meal and the fish loses a parasite which it would be unable to dislodge on its own.

Q What simple animal is destroying the Great Barrier Reef?

A The crown of thorns starfish (below) lives in tropical seas. It is common on the Great Barrier Reef off the coast of Australia. It turns its stomach inside out to eat the soft-bodied coral animals. Its skin is armored with fearsome spines and it has few predators. The crown of thorns has destroyed large areas of coral reef.

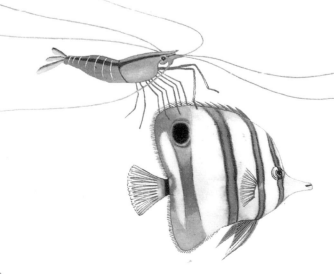

INSECTS & SPIDERS

Q How does the praying mantis get its name?

A The praying mantis (below) is a fierce, predatory insect that catches other insects for food. Its front pair of legs are specially adapted for grabbing prey. As the mantis is stalking its victim, these legs are held folded under its head. When it does this, it looks as though it might be praying, and this is how it got its name.

Q Which is the most poisonous spider?

A Although quite small, the black widow (above) is perhaps the most deadly spider. There are several different species which live in warm areas such as North America and Australia. Because it likes dark, shady places, the spider often goes into houses. It is therefore more likely to bite people than other poisonous spiders.

Q How do ants live?

A Ants are insects that live in colonies. Their large underground nests (right) contain thousands of individual ants, and have a series of chambers and tunnels. One important chamber will be home to the queen ant. She lays thousands of eggs which soon hatch into ant larvae. These are first fed by the adult ants. Then they turn into pupae from which adult ants finally emerge.

Queen ant

Eggs

Worker ants keep greenfly for food

Worker ant

Larvae

Adult ants break out of pupae

Worker ant bringing food

Plain tiger butterfly

Hawk moth

Atlas moth

Q Do insects have territories?

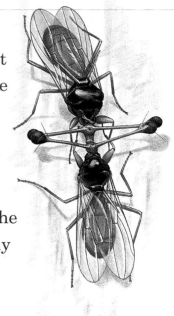

A A few insects do have territories which they defend against others of their kind. These two male stalk-eyed flies (right) from Africa are assessing each other's size by measuring their eye stalks. The prize for the winner is to mate with any female that enters the territory.

Q How can you tell butterflies and moths apart?

A Although similar insects to look at, butterflies fly by day while moths mostly fly at night. Most butterflies have club-tipped antennae while moths usually have straight or feathery antennae (above). Butterflies usually close their wings together at rest.

Q How many different kinds of insects are there?

A Nobody knows for sure how many different insects there are. It has been estimated, however, that there may be more than 30 million types, or species, in a huge variety of shapes and sizes. Examples from the major groups, or orders, of insects are shown below.

Q Why are some insects brightly colored?

A Some insects have bright colors to attract one another to mate. Others, such as this ladybird, advertise the fact that they taste nasty by being colorful. Birds and other predators soon learn to associate the color red in particular with creatures which taste nasty or which may be poisonous.

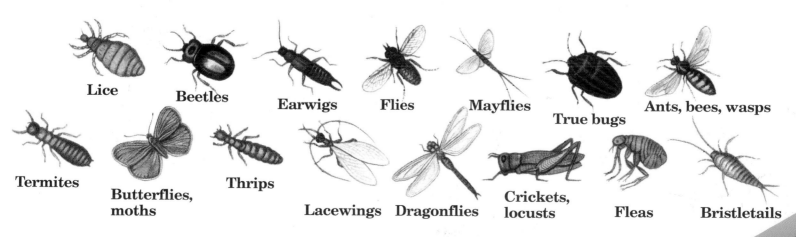

Lice

Beetles

Earwigs

Flies

Mayflies

True bugs

Ants, bees, wasps

Termites

Butterflies, moths

Thrips

Lacewings

Dragonflies

Crickets, locusts

Fleas

Bristletails

FISH

Which fish
climbs trees?

The mudskipper (below) lives in
African mangrove swamps. Because it
can take in oxygen through its mouth and
throat, it can venture on to the
mudflats when the tide is out.
If danger threatens and
it cannot get back to
its burrow, it can
climb mangrove
roots to escape.

Q What is unusual
about the seahorse?

A Apart from its curious
shape, the seahorse
(right) is unusual because it is
the male and not the female which
looks after the eggs and young. He has a brood
pouch on his belly and this can hold up to 200
eggs and young. When the young are old
enough, the male expels them from the pouch.

Q How does a fish sense its surroundings?

A Although most fish have good eyesight and a sense of
taste, they also use a structure called the lateral line
(right). This groove lies along the side of a fish's body, and
contains special cells that are sensitive to vibrations in the
water. With this, the fish can detect both food and danger.

Lateral line

Q How does a shark hunt its prey?

A Although sharks have
poor eyesight, they have
an excellent sense of smell. They
can detect blood diluted a million
times in water and will home in on a
wounded animal in the sea. Sharks
are also able to detect vibrations in
the water caused, for example, by
the thrashing movements of an
injured fish.

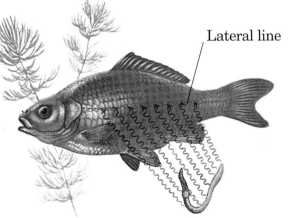

Q Which fish
can spear boats?

A Although they do not do it often,
swordfish (right) have been known to
spear the hulls of wooden boats. They have a
snout which is long and pointed. It carries rows of
small, sharp teeth along the sides, rather like the
blade of a saw. The swordfish probably uses this to slash at prey and predators.

Q How do butterfly fish get their
name?

A Butterfly fish get their name
because they are very brightly
colored, like the wings of a butterfly. Most
species are found on coral reefs in tropical
waters around the world. The colors and
patterns are thought to confuse predators.
They may also help the fish blend into its
surroundings to hide from predators.

Q How does a flounder avoid its
enemies?

A The flounder (below) is a flatfish
that lives on the sandy seabed. Its
markings and colors help it blend in
with its surroundings, for camouflage.
The flounder can also flick
sand over its body using
its fins.
Often only
the head
and eyes
remain visible.

AMPHIBIANS & REPTILES

Q Are all snakes poisonous?

A Many snakes are perfectly harmless to humans and do not have poison fangs or venom. Although it may look menacing, this Arafura wart snake (above), which lives in rivers in Australia and New Guinea, does not have a poisonous bite.

Q What is a salamander?

A Salamanders such as this tiger salamander (right) are related to newts, and both are amphibians. Salamanders are perfectly at home on land but have to live in damp places. This is because their skins easily lose water. Some species can breed on land but many return to water to spawn. Salamanders eat small creatures such as worms and slugs.

Q How do frogs breathe?

A Like other amphibians, frogs have lungs which they use to take in air and absorb oxygen into their blood. They are also able to take up oxygen through their skins. In order to do this, however, they have to keep their bodies moist at all times. Frogs are also able to absorb oxygen through the moist lining of their mouths.

Q Which turtle travels farthest?

A Most turtles travel long distances during their lives. The green turtle (left), however, probably holds the record. Individuals that feed off the coast of South America travel 1,360 miles to Ascension Island to breed. Turtles make these long-distance journeys because the number of beaches suitable for egg-laying is small.

Q How does the collared lizard escape?

A The collared lizard (right) lives on grassy plains in North America. In order to escape from danger, the lizard is able to run on its back legs. It is able, therefore, to move at faster speeds than if it were having to scurry on all four legs.

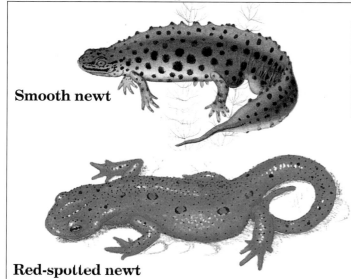

Smooth newt

Red-spotted newt

Q How do newts find their way home?

A Newts such as the smooth newt and the red-spotted newt spend much of their lives on land but return to water to breed. They often find the pond where they themselves were spawned. Most species use taste and smell to help them navigate. A few species also use the Sun or the Earth's magnetism to check the direction they are traveling in.

Q Which reptiles can change color?

A Chameleons (left) are able to change their color to match their background. They do this by moving pigment around in their skins, and the change can be complete in just a few minutes. Chameleons use this ability to change color for camouflage. This way they can avoid being spotted by predators. They can also get closer to prey without being seen.

NATURE

BIRDS

Q Why are birds' beaks different?

A Each bird species has a beak whose shape is best suited to the way it feeds. Birds of prey (1) have hooked beaks for tearing flesh, while waders (2) have long beaks for probing the mud for worms. Kookaburras (3) have stabbing beaks for catching reptiles, while nightjars (4) have wide gapes to catch flying insects. Puffins (5) use their beaks both for catching food and to send signals.

Q Why do vultures have bald heads?

A Vultures (right) feed on the carcasses of dead animals. They sometimes have to push their heads inside the body in order to get a meal. If they had feathers on their heads and necks, these would soon become clogged and matted with blood.

Q Which bird is the pirate of the air?

A Frigatebirds are large seabirds that live in the tropics. Instead of catching their own food, they behave like pirates towards other birds. When a frigatebird sees a bird such as a booby returning from a fishing trip, it gives chase. It pulls the victim's tail and wings until it drops its food. The frigatebird then catches the fish in mid-air.

Booby

Frigatebird

Q What is a cockatoo?

A Cockatoos are a type of parrot. They can raise their head feathers to form a crest. Most species come from Australia and New Guinea. The palm cockatoo is the largest cockatoo and also the largest Australian parrot. It lives in rainforests. The galah is sometimes called the roseate cockatoo and also comes from Australia. It is the most common cockatoo and lives near farmland.

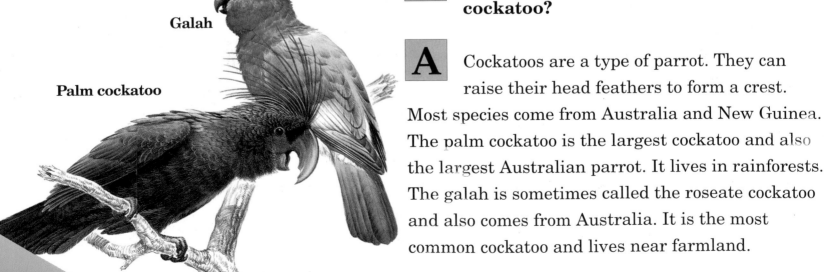

Galah

Palm cockatoo

Q How many feathers does a bird have?

A The number of feathers on a bird varies according to the species, its age and the season. Most small songbirds have between 1,500 and 3,000 feathers on their bodies. A swan, however, might have as many as 25,000 feathers. A bird of prey, such as this eagle (left), would have between 5–8,000 feathers.

Q How does a woodpecker find its food?

A Woodpeckers (below) have large, chisel-like bills and a strong skull. When they tap the trunk of a tree, they can tell if an insect grub is living inside by the sound the tapping makes. When they find a likely spot, they smash open the wood with heavy blows from the bill. They can then take the insect to eat.

Q How did the secretary bird get its name?

A Secretary birds (right) have strange-looking feathers arranged on their heads. When the first explorers visited Africa and saw these birds they reminded them of Victorian secretaries who used to keep their quill pens behind their ears. Secretary birds catch snakes with their long legs.

SEA MAMMALS

Bottle-nosed dolphin

Common porpoise

Q What is the difference between a dolphin and a porpoise?

A A dolphin is larger than a porpoise (above) and has a beak-nose; it also has a large hump on its forehead. The porpoise is the smallest of the whales and does not have the dolphin's "beak." Instead it has a rather stubby, rounded head. Dolphins and porpoises are both types of small whale. They feed on fish and can swim very fast to catch their prey.

Q Which animal is called the sea canary?

A The beluga whale (above), which lives in arctic seas, is called the sea canary. This is because it makes a wide variety of clicking and chirping noises and sometimes snaps its jaws together as well. In the summer, belugas move into the mouths of rivers to feed on migrating salmon. They sometimes gather in large numbers to feed, and their canary-like sounds can be heard from above the water as well as from below. Adult belugas are white but their young are darker in color.

Q How did the right whale get its name?

A Sad though it may seem, early whalers gave the right whale its name. They considered it to be the "right" whale to catch because it was a slow swimmer and floated after it had been killed. Some species of whale sink after they have been killed and would have been difficult for early whalers to tow back to their ship. Right whales were nearly hunted to extinction.

Q Which is the most ferocious sea mammal?

A The killer whale (below) is the most ferocious sea mammal. It eats fish, squid, sharks and even seals, porpoises and walruses. Sometimes killer whales launch themselves from the sea to snatch seals from the beach. Packs of killer whales have even been known to attack animals as large as blue whales. Surprisingly, attacks on humans have never been known, and killer whales can be watched closely from boats.

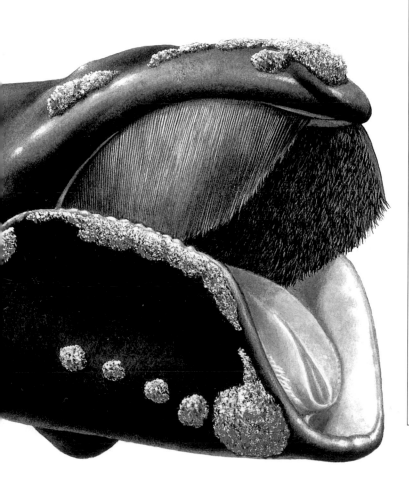

Q How does the sea otter eat clams?

A The sea otter lives in the north Pacific waters off California. It has developed a clever method of opening clams and mussel shells to reach the food inside. Lying on its back on the surface of the sea, the sea otter places a large stone on its chest. It then strikes the clam or mussel shell against the stone until the shell shatters. The sea otter can then easily reach the food inside the shell.

NATURE

Q Which animal is called the "walking pine cone"?

A This name is used to describe the pangolin (left). It is also sometimes called the scaly anteater. Most of the pangolin's body is covered in hard, protective, overlapping scales. When threatened, it curls into a ball. Some pangolins can climb trees.

Q Which animal is called the river horse?

A The hippopotamus (above) is sometimes called the river horse. In fact its name is made up of Greek and Latin words meaning "river" and "horse." Hippos live in Africa and spend much of the day partly under the water in rivers and lakes. After dark, they may come out to feed on the plants on the bank. Hippos can be quarrelsome animals and two males will often fight one another, sometimes causing injuries.

Q What is a rhino's horn made from?

A Although it may look solid and bony, the horn of a rhino (below) has a hollow center and is made from the same material as hair and hooves. Rhinos are sometimes illegally killed for their horns, in the belief that the horn makes a good medicine. As a result, rhinos are rare and endangered today even though the trade in their horns is banned in most countries.

Q How does a mongoose defeat a cobra?

A The deadly cobra is usually no match for a mongoose. The mongoose is extremely agile, and leaps away when the snake tries to strike. Soon the snake tires, and then the mongoose attacks, killing the snake with a bite to the neck.

Q How does a lion catch its prey?

A Although its prey may be fast-moving, a lion is stealthy and will creep close to its victim before making its attack. Lions often work as a team with different individuals cutting off the prey's line of escape. Animals such as this wildebeest (right) are sometimes killed with a bite to the neck which crushes the vertebrae. On other occasions, the lion suffocates its prey by gripping on to the throat.

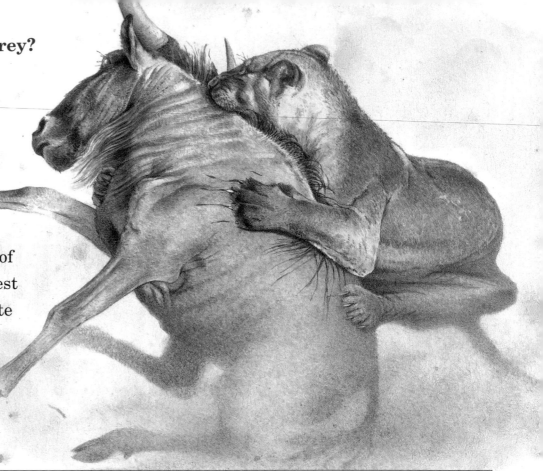

Q How do kangaroos and wallabies run?

A Kangaroos and wallabies run using their large and powerful back legs to hop. The small front legs are used only for feeding and grooming. The long, robust tail helps the animal balance when it is hopping. Some kangaroos can reach speeds of 25 mph or more and are able to hop for long periods of time. Kangaroos live in Australia.

Q How does the porcupine protect itself?

A The sharp, spiny quills of a porcupine are really just specially strengthened hairs. In some species, such as the African porcupine (left), they can reach a length of 20 inches. The quills are so strong that they can cause painful injuries if they are jabbed into a would-be attacker.

NATURE

ANIMAL BEHAVIOR

Q How do musk ox protect their young?

A When threatened by enemies, such as wolves, a herd of musk ox (right) form a line facing them, or form a circle with the calves in the middle (below). Big males then dash out and jab the attackers with their huge, powerful, curved horns.

Q Why do some animals only come out at night?

A Animals that only come out at night are called nocturnal. They may be nocturnal in order to catch other nocturnal animals or to avoid daytime predators, or both. Nocturnal animals often have large eyes and good eyesight. They also need a keen sense of smell and good hearing to listen for danger.

Q How do chimps show their moods?

A Scientists have shown that chimps (left) show their moods through their facial expressions. The shape of the mouth, and whether or not the teeth are bared, are important signals. From top to bottom, the chimps are showing a desire to play, begging for food, intense fear and, lastly, anxiety.

Q How does the honeyguide get its name?

A Honeyguides (below) come from Africa and are so-called because they lead honey badgers and humans to the nests of wild bees using a series of calls. After the nest has been raided for honey, the honeyguide gets the chance to feed on bee grubs from the open nest.

Q How are young cuckoos reared?

A Female cuckoos (below) lay their eggs in the nests of other birds and then abandon their offspring. The host bird has the task of feeding and rearing the young cuckoo. As it grows up, the young cuckoo tips the host bird's eggs and young from the nest. By the time it is ready to leave the nest, the young cuckoo may be several times the size of its long-suffering foster parent.

Q Why do animals defend their territory?

A Not all animals have territories but many do. If food is limited, the animal may defend a territory to guard its food supply. With other species, such as these cassowaries (right), the males fight over a territory in which to nest and rear their young. Territorial animals know exactly where the boundaries of their own territory lie.

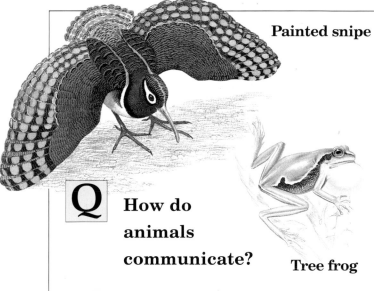

Painted snipe

Tree frog

Q How do animals communicate?

A Animals signal to each other in two main ways: by using visual signals, such as shape or color, and by sound. Birds, such as the painted snipe, have showy wings which they fan out to make an impression. Many birds sing to advertise their territories or attract a mate. Most frogs can also produce a croaking song to mark their territories or attract a mate.

NATURE

FARM ANIMALS

Q What is the most popular cart-horse?

A The Percheron (left) is the most popular cart-horse breed in the world. It is named after Perche, the region of France where it was first developed and used. Standing more than 16.1 hands high, this gentle giant can pull immense loads without much effort. It was originally used for pulling heavy loads but today is just as popular as a show horse.

Q How are beef and dairy cattle different?

A Dairy cattle, such as this Friesian and Dairy Shorthorn, are lighter in build than beef cattle. The udders are big so that they can hold large volumes of milk. Before a dairy cow can produce milk, she has to give birth to a calf. After the birth, she continues to produce milk for up to 10 months or so. Dairy cows are usually milked twice a day.

Berkshire

Duroc

Q What meats do pigs provide?

A Pigs are reared for their meat which is either eaten fresh as pork, or in cured form as bacon and ham. Different pig breeds serve different needs. The Duroc, Berkshire and Saddleback are pork breeds while the Tamworth is a bacon breed.

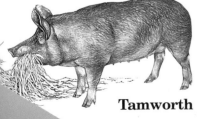

Tamworth

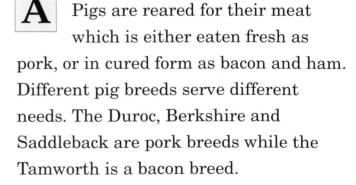

Saddleback

Q Why are there different cattle breeds?

A Different breeds of cattle are suited to different climates around the world. The most successful breed of beef cattle is the Hereford. It is ideal for cool climates. For hot climates, breeds such as the Kankrej are ideal. It is popular in India. The Santa Gertrudis also thrives in hot places and is widely farmed in Texas.

Santa Gertrudis

Kankrej

Hereford

Q Why do people raise chickens?

A People keep chickens (right) for three main reasons: for their meat, for their eggs and lastly for show. There are many different breeds. The Leghorn is the best egg-laying breed while the Barnvelder is kept for meat.

Leghorn   Barnvelder

Q How long have people kept goats?

A Goats (right) have been kept as herd animals for at least 9,000 years. They are bred for a variety of purposes. Their meat and skins are both useful and in some countries goats are used to carry loads. In many countries, goat numbers are very high and they damage wild plant life by overgrazing.

Q What is sheep wool used for?

A The quality of sheep wool varies from breed to breed and can be used for a range of purposes. The wool from the German Blackface is fine and makes excellent cloth. That from the Corriedale is coarse and springy and is used for tweeds and carpets.

Corriedale

German Blackface

PETS

Q Where do canaries come from?

A In the wild, canaries (above) are found on the Canary Islands off North Africa and the islands of the Azores and Madeira. They have been kept for more than 400 years because they can sing. Breeding in captivity has produced a wide range of different colors. Most captive birds are bright yellow. Their wild relatives are a duller olive-green color and are still found on their native islands.

Q Do pet mice have wild relatives?

A Domesticated pet mice are all descended from the wild house mouse. This animal has lived alongside humans for more than 10,000 years, ever since people began to store grain and other foods. Mice have been kept as pets for several centuries and a range of color varieties (right) has been bred.

Q What is a Manx cat?

A The Manx cat (above) is a very distinctive breed that is best known for its lack of tail. It first came from the Isle of Man, an island in the Irish Sea. Manx cats have long legs for their size with thickset bodies. Their color is like that of a tabby or wild cat, with stripes and blotches of various shades of brown and gray-brown. Manx cats are popular as a show breed but they do not make particularly affectionate pets.

Q How many breeds of dogs are there?

A There are over 300 different breeds of dogs, and each country has its own system of grouping them. In the UK and Australia the main groups are: hounds, terriers, toys, gun, working and utility. In America they also group dogs into sporting and nonsporting. European countries use different groupings.

Bouvier des Flandres (working)

American foxhound (hound)

Q **Are there different breeds of rabbit?**

A There are many different breeds and varieties of rabbit, all descended from the wild rabbit. About 2,000 years ago, the Romans brought rabbits from their native Spain, Portugal and southern France to raise them for their meat. Rabbits now live in many parts of the world. People also breed rabbits for their fur and for show.

Q **What is a Persian cat?**

A A Persian (right) is the best-known breed of long-haired cat. It was first bred in Europe in the 1800s by crossing cats imported from Persia (now Iran) and from Angora in Turkey. The breed has a long, silky coat and a broad head. A Persian cat's legs are short but the body is broad and robust. Although this example is black-and-white, Persians come in several different colors.

Irish setter (gundog)

Great dane (utility)

Lakeland terrier (terrier)

Chihuahua (toy)

NATURE

PLANT KINGDOM

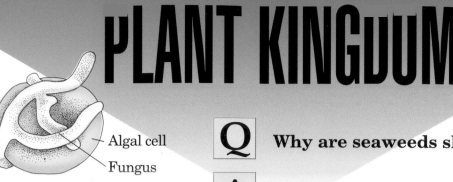

— Algal cell
— Fungus

Q What are lichens?

A Lichens (above) are curious plants. They are made up of algal cells, surrounded by a fungus. The same algae can live alone but the fungus needs the algae to survive, because the algae can make food from sunlight energy. Lichens live on stones and trees and grow slowly.

Q Why are seaweeds slimy?

A Seaweeds (right) are simple plants that grow on the seashore. There are lots of different types but most feel slimy to the touch. This is because there is a thin, jelly-like layer on the seaweed surface. The jelly-like layer prevents the seaweed from being damaged by the waves.

Q What are fungi?

A Fungi belong to a group of organisms separate from plants and animals. Unlike plants, they have no green pigment and cannot make their own food. The main part of a large fungus is a huge network of tiny threads in the ground. These take up food from the soil or from dead plants and animals. At certain times of year, spore-producing mushrooms and toadstools like those shown here emerge.

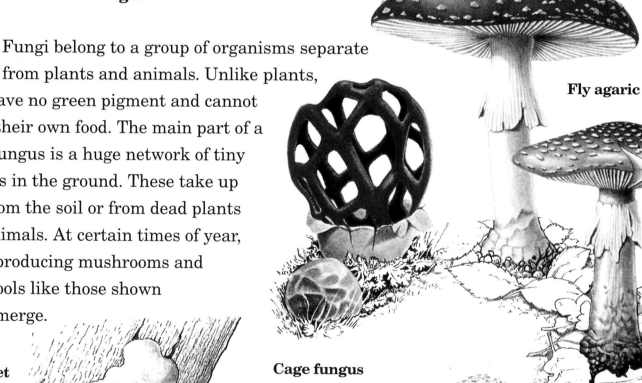

Fly agaric

Blusher

Bracket fungus

Cage fungus

Earthball

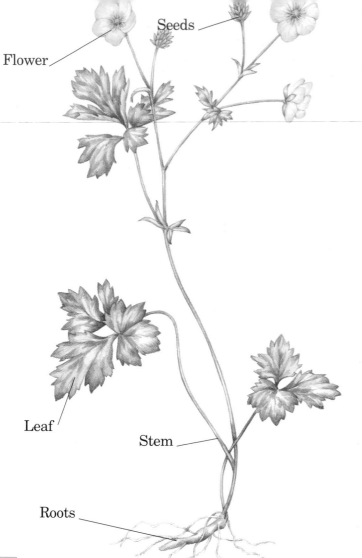

Flower

Seeds

Leaf

Stem

Roots

Q Which plants produce cones?

A Plants that produce cones are called conifers (below). Conifers often grow as large trees which are themselves cone-shaped in outline. Cones are the parts of the conifer used for reproduction, so there are male and female cones. Male cones produce pollen which is carried by the wind to fertilize the female cone. This then develops and matures. Seeds form between the hard, protective scales of the cone and are released when ripe.

Pine cone

Fir cone

Conifer tree

Q What are the parts of a flowering plant called?

A A flowering plant (above) usually has roots anchoring it in the soil. These take up water and nutrients. Above ground, a stem carries these to the leaves. The leaves use sunlight energy to make food. At the ends of the stem are flowers, the reproductive parts. Oncc fcrtilized, the flowers produce seeds.

Q How is timber cut from a tree trunk?

A A felled tree trunk is first stripped of its branches. It is then cut lengthways in an ordered way so that no timber is wasted. First, two sides of the trunk are cut to produce thin planks of wood. Then the central part of the tree trunk is cut into thicker lengths of wood suitable for building work.

NATURE

PLANT LIFE

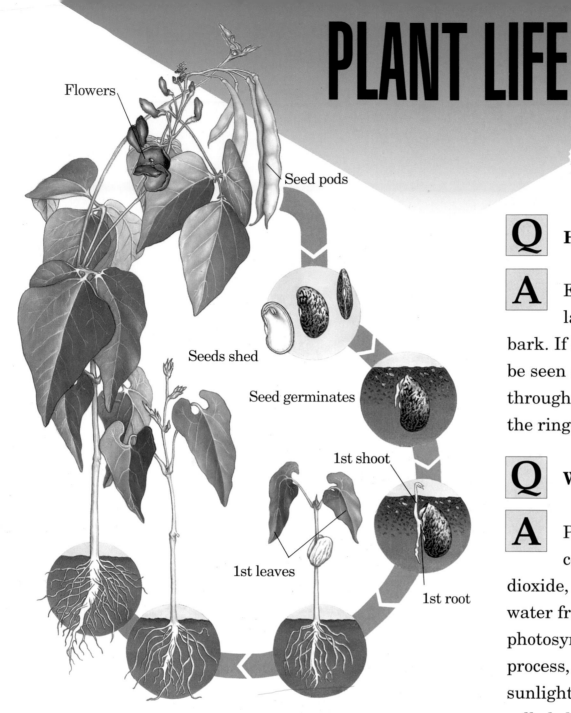

Flowers

Seed pods

Seeds shed

Seed germinates

1st shoot

1st leaves

1st root

How can you tell a tree's age?

A Every year a tree grows a new layer of wood just beneath the bark. If a tree is cut down, the layers can be seen as rings in the cross-section through the stump (above). By counting the rings you can tell its age.

Q **Why do plants need sunlight?**

A Plants make their own food by combining a gas called carbon dioxide, which they get from the air, with water from the soil. This process is called photosynthesis (below). To power the process, the plant uses the energy of sunlight. A green pigment in the leaves called chlorophyll traps the Sun's energy.

Q **How does a plant complete its life cycle?**

A Every year, plants (above) produce large numbers of seeds which fall to the ground. Many die but some will germinate. Tiny roots and shoots grow from the seed and soon the plant increases in size. As the plant grows larger, more and more leaves are produced and eventually flowers appear. Pollen from male flowers fertilizes female flowers and the base of the flower begins to swell. It is here that this year's seeds are being made, completing the plant's life cycle.

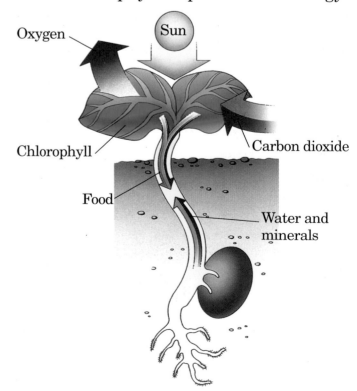

Oxygen

Sun

Chlorophyll

Carbon dioxide

Food

Water and minerals

Q Which plants eat animals?

A Venus fly traps and pitcher plants
(right) can absorb nutrients from
animals. Venus fly traps have leaves which
trap insects and digest them. Pitcher plants
have flask-shaped leaves in which water
collects. Insects fall in and drown.

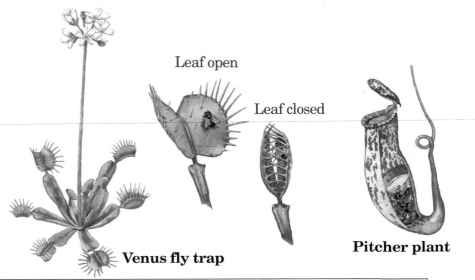

Leaf open

Leaf closed

Venus fly trap

Pitcher plant

Q What are fruit "pips"?

A Fruit pips are the seeds of the
plant which produced the fruit.
There are many types of fruit but most
are juicy and nutritious, which make
animals eat them. The seed may be swallowed whole and
passed out in the animal's droppings later on. In this way,
the plant has its seeds scattered, or dispersed.

Q Why do plants produce flowers?

A Plants produce flowers (below) to reproduce and
create a new generation. Flowers bear the male
and female parts. Many flowers
have colors and scents that
attract insects. The insects
take male pollen to the
female parts of other
flowers. The pollen of
some flowers is
carried by the wind.

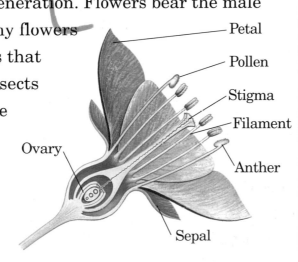

Petal

Pollen

Stigma

Filament

Ovary

Anther

Sepal

Q How do daffodils survive the winter?

A Daffodils have leaves and
flowers above ground only
for a few months each
spring. During the winter
they live as onion-
shaped bulbs buried
in the ground. Bulbs are
protected from
winter frosts
by the soil
above them.

Bulb cross-section

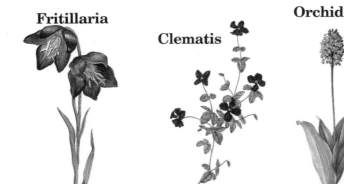

Silver birch

Fritillaria

Clematis

Orchid

NATURE

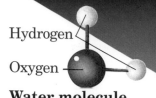
CHEMICALS & MATTER

Hydrogen

Oxygen

Water molecule

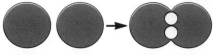

Oxygen atoms   Oxygen molecule

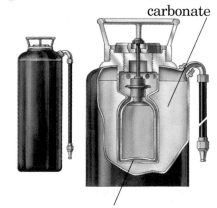

Q What are molecules?

A A molecule (above) is the simplest part of a substance that can take part in chemical reactions. It is a group of two or more atoms linked together. The atoms may be the same or different. For example, a molecule of water is made of two hydrogen atoms linked to an oxygen atom. An oxygen molecule is made of two oxygen atoms linked together.

Q What is the difference between a mixture and a compound?

A If iron filings and sulfur (1) are mixed together (2), there is no chemical reaction and they can be separated again by removing the iron with a magnet (3). When iron filings and sulfur are heated (4) they combine and change into iron sulfide, a compound.

Q What chemicals are used in fire extinguishers?

A Carbon dioxide extinguishers send out a jet of carbon dioxide gas. Dry powder extinguishers blanket a fire with powder. Soda-acid extinguishers (right) mix sulfuric acid with sodium carbonate, making carbon dioxide gas which forces out a jet of water.

Sodium carbonate

Sulfuric acid

Q How do soaps and detergents work?

A Soaps and detergents are made from long molecules that are water-loving at one end and grease-loving at the other end. When they go to work on dirty cloth, they surround each droplet of greasy dirt stuck to the fibers of the cloth with their grease-loving tails plugged into the grease droplet (below). The coated droplet then floats off the cloth into the water and is washed away.

Grease

Cloth

1

2

3

4

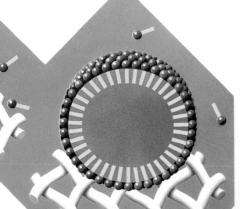

Q How are chemicals made?

A The chemical industry makes chemicals by processing raw materials with heat, pressure and chemical reactions. Sulfuric acid is made from sulfur in a series of stages (right) that change sulfur into different compounds, ending with sulfuric acid.

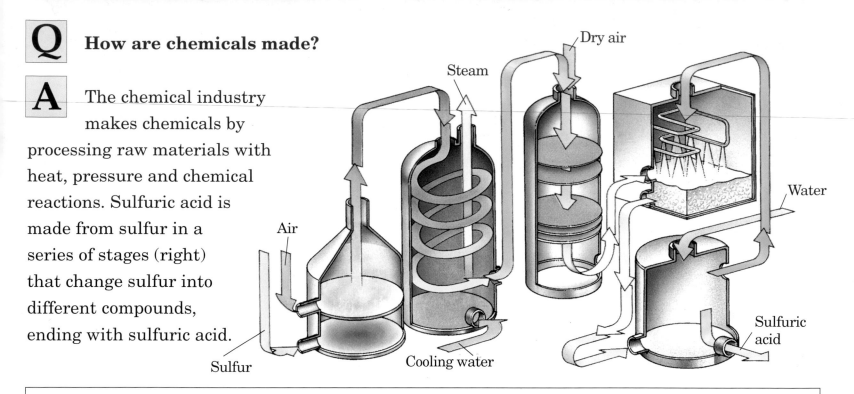

Steam

Dry air

Air

Water

Sulfur

Cooling water

Sulfuric acid

Q What are crystals?

A Crystals are solid pieces of material with flat faces set at angles to each other. All crystals of the same substance have the same angles between their faces. Crystals form in this way because their atoms always lie in the same regular patterns. Salt, sugar and quartz are crystals. Minerals can sometimes be identified by the shape of their crystals.

Q What is chemical analysis?

A Chemists use chemical analysis (right) to find out what an unknown substance contains. There are several methods. Volumetric analysis involves reactions in solutions. Gravimetric analysis involves weighing. In gas-liquid chromatography, gas carries the sample through a column of moist powder. The sample separates into simpler compounds that are recorded on a chart as they leave the column.

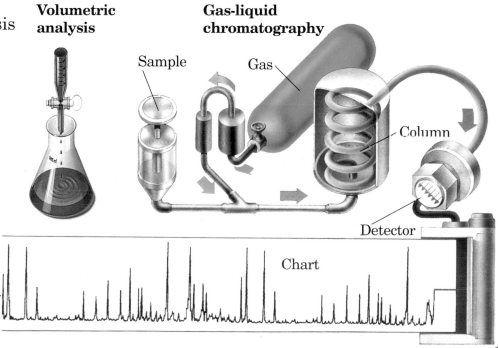

Volumetric analysis

Gas-liquid chromatography

Sample

Gas

Column

Detector

Chart

SCIENCE & TECHNOLOGY

MATERIALS

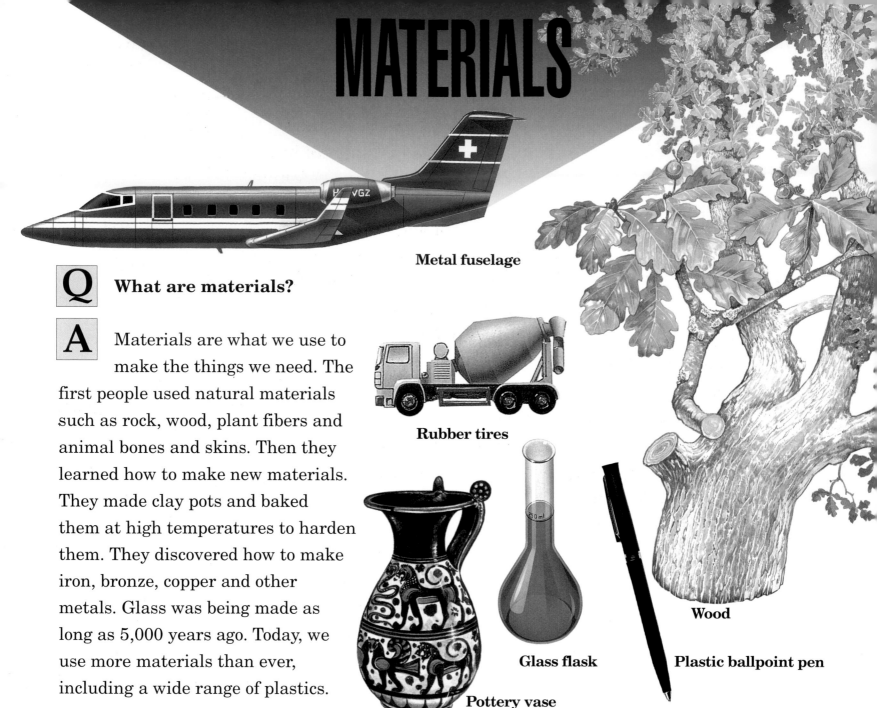

Metal fuselage

Rubber tires

Glass flask

Wood

Plastic ballpoint pen

Pottery vase

Q What are materials?

A Materials are what we use to make the things we need. The first people used natural materials such as rock, wood, plant fibers and animal bones and skins. Then they learned how to make new materials. They made clay pots and baked them at high temperatures to harden them. They discovered how to make iron, bronze, copper and other metals. Glass was being made as long as 5,000 years ago. Today, we use more materials than ever, including a wide range of plastics.

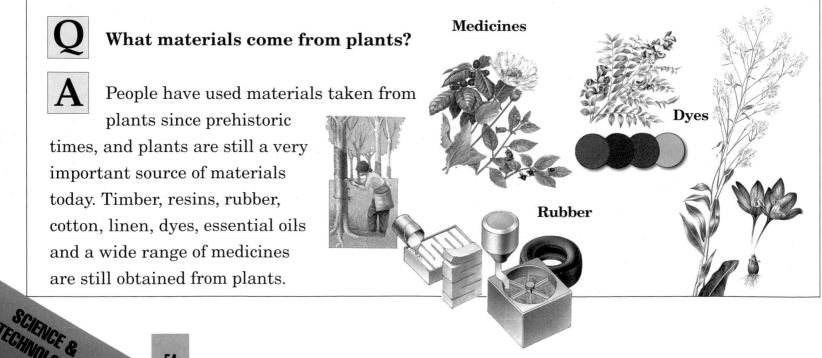

Medicines

Dyes

Rubber

Q What materials come from plants?

A People have used materials taken from plants since prehistoric times, and plants are still a very important source of materials today. Timber, resins, rubber, cotton, linen, dyes, essential oils and a wide range of medicines are still obtained from plants.

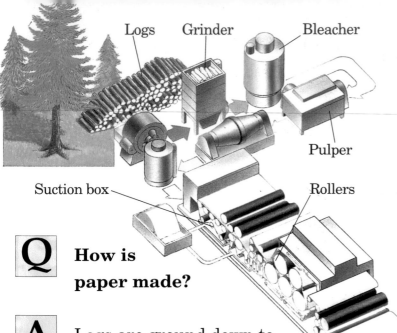

Logs   Grinder   Bleacher

Pulper

Suction box

Rollers

Q How is paper made?

A Logs are ground down to form a watery pulp. The pulp is poured on to wire mesh. Water is sucked and rolled out, leaving a thin film of paper. The process is continuous. Pulp is fed into one end of the machine (above) and paper comes out at the other end.

Paper

Q What are composites?

A Composites are materials made by combining two or more materials. Many kinds of boats (above) are made by laying mats of glass fibers into a mold and then soaking the mats in liquid plastic. The plastic sets hard and is reinforced by the fibers to make a smooth, tough, lightweight hull.

Q What do we get from crude oil?

A Crude oil is separated into materials ranging from bitumen for road-making to fuels such as gasoline and heating gas. Crude oil is heated inside a tall fractionating tower (right). Gas and light fuels evaporate and collect near the top of the tower, leaving heavier oils and bitumen to settle at the bottom.

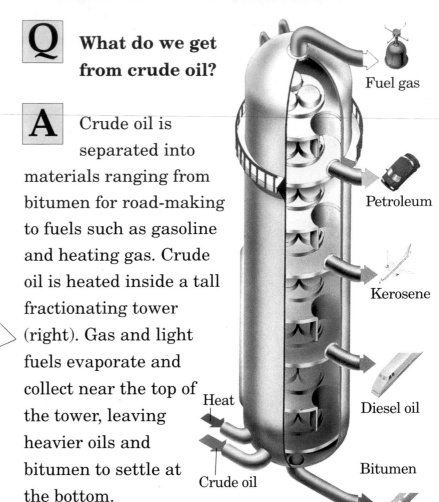

Fuel gas

Petroleum

Kerosene

Heat

Diesel oil

Crude oil

Bitumen

Q How is plastic recycled?

A Waste plastic is loaded into a furnace (below) and heated. The gas given off is then separated in a distillation column. Wax and tar collect at the bottom, while lighter gases collect farther up. Some of the gas is fed back to fuel the furnace.

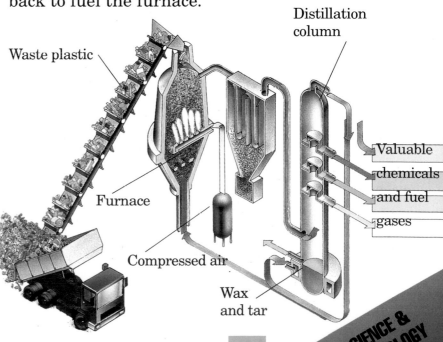

Distillation column

Waste plastic

Furnace

Valuable chemicals and fuel gases

Compressed air

Wax and tar

SCIENCE & TECHNOLOGY

FORCES & ENERGY

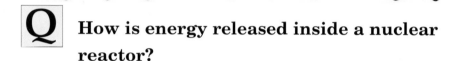

Slow-moving neutron

Uranium-235

Uranium-236

Fission fragment   Fission fragment
                    Uranium-235

Q What is gravity?

A Gravity is the force that pulls everything to Earth. Galileo showed that gravity makes all objects fall equally fast. When he dropped a light ball and a heavy ball from the leaning Tower of Pisa (above), they hit the ground at the same instant.

Q What is an Archimedes' Screw used for?

A The Archimedes' Screw (below) was invented by Archimedes in Ancient Greece. It is used for lifting water. One end of the screw is dipped into water. By turning the handle, the water is raised up inside the tube until it spills out of the top.

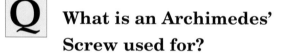

Q How is energy released inside a nuclear reactor?

A A slow-moving neutron is made to hit an atom of uranium-235 (above). It combines with the nucleus at the center of the atom, forming uranium-236. This splits into two particles called fission fragments, releasing a burst of energy and three more neutrons, which split more uranium atoms.

Q What forces act on an airplane in flight?

A Four forces act on an airplane. Its weight acts downwards. The thrust of its engines pushes it forwards. Lift created by its wings acts upwards. Drag tries to slow it down. Thrust must overcome drag, and lift must overcome weight, if a plane is to fly.

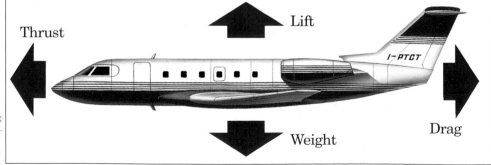

Thrust   Lift

Weight   Drag

Q How does a space rocket work?

A A rocket motor propels a rocket by burning fuel mixed with an oxidizer. The oxidizer contains oxygen, which is necessary for burning. The Ariane V rocket (below), burns hydrogen fuel with oxygen. The hot gas produced rushes out of the motor nozzles, forcing the rocket upwards.

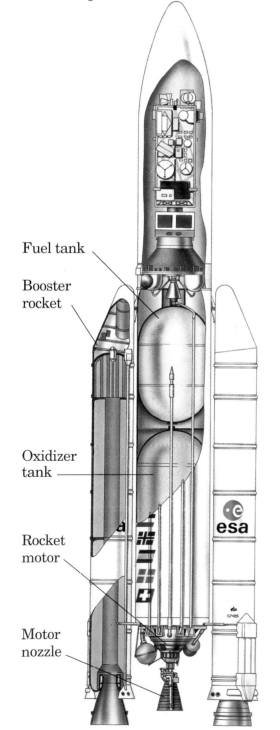

Fuel tank

Booster rocket

esa

Oxidizer tank

Rocket motor

Motor nozzle

Q What is a force?

A A force is something that changes an object's speed or direction. Forces always exist in pairs acting in opposite directions. When a rifle is fired (below right), the rifle kicks back as the bullet flies forwards. A heavier football player running faster applies a greater force than a lighter, slower player (below left).

Q What is friction?

A Friction is a force that stops surfaces sliding across each other easily. Sometimes friction is helpful. It allows our shoes to grip the ground. Without friction walking would be impossible. But friction can also be a problem because it wears out the moving parts of machines.

Q How does a turbine work?

A A turbine (right) is a machine that uses gas or liquid to make a shaft turn. Water hitting the buckets of a Pelton wheel drives the buckets around and turns the shaft. Wind spins the blades of a wind turbine. Wind and water turbines often drive electricity generators.

Wind turbine

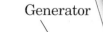

Rotor blade

Generator

Pelton wheel

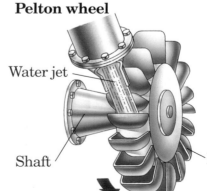

Water jet

Shaft

Buckets

SCIENCE & TECHNOLOGY

SOUND

Direction of wave →

Rarefaction   Compression   Rarefaction

Q What is sound?

A Sound is a form of energy. Sound is made when something vibrates in air. The vibrations push against the surrounding air molecules, forming a sound wave. First the air molecules are squeezed (this is called compression), then they are stretched (this is called rarefaction). It is easiest to think of sound waves moving in the same way as a wave of energy moves along a coil of spring if one end is moved up and down (above).

Q How do we hear sounds?

A When sound waves reach us, the outer ear channels them inside the ear, where they make the eardrum vibrate. The vibrations are magnified 20 times by the hammer, anvil, and stirrup bones, causing liquid to vibrate inside a tube called the cochlea (right). Nerves in the cochlea pass messages to the brain, enabling us to recognise the sound.

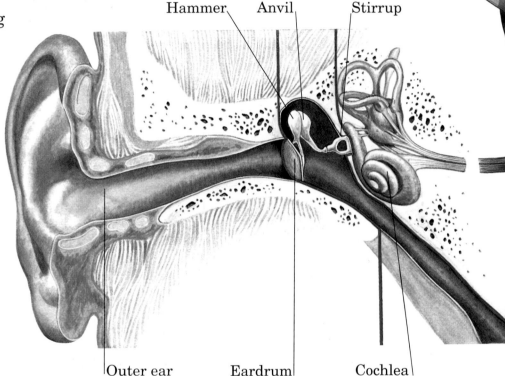
Hammer   Anvil   Stirrup

Outer ear   Eardrum   Cochlea

Q How fast does sound travel?

A Sound travels through solids, liquids and gases at different speeds. Its speed depends on the density of the material. It travels faster through dense materials like steel than through less dense materials like air (below).

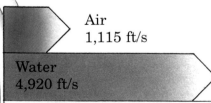

Air
1,115 ft/s

Water
4,920 ft/s

Concrete
16,495 ft/s

Steel
19,685 ft/s

Q How is loudness measured?

A Loudness depends on the amount of energy carried by a sound wave. The loudness of sound is measured in decibels (dB). Sounds louder than 120dB can damage the ears. Sounds louder than 130dB cause pain. Some animals, like bats, make sounds that we cannot hear at all (below).

Decibels 140   Pain threshold

130

100

70

40

0

Q Why does the sound of a racing car engine change as it drives past us?

A As the racing car (right) approaches, the sound waves in front of it get squashed together. These short sound waves make the engine's noise sound high pitched. As the car moves past, the sound waves become stretched out behind it. The longer waves make the engine's note sound lower.

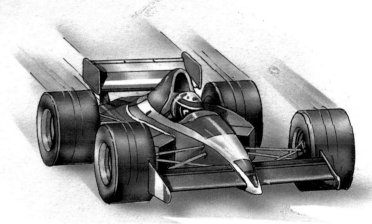

Q How does sound travel down telephone wires?

A A carbon block in the mouthpiece converts the sound pressure waves of the caller's voice into electrical signals. These flow along wires (below) to the telephone at the other end. The magnet in the earpiece converts the signals back into sound pressure waves.

Magnet

Carbon block

SCIENCE & TECHNOLOGY

ELECTRICITY & MAGNETISM

Q How do electric vehicles work?

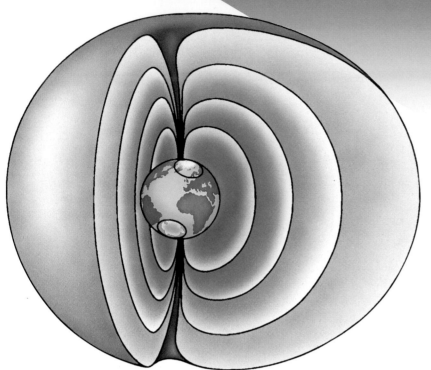

A An electric car (above) works by using electricity stored in batteries to power an electric motor connected to the car's wheels. Electric trains are supplied with electricity from wires above the track or a third rail beside the track. It powers electric motors that turn the wheels.

Q What is a magnetic field?

A A magnetic field is a region of forces that exists around a magnet. The field can be drawn as a series of curved lines, called lines of force, joining the magnet's north and south poles. The Earth behaves like a magnet. Its magnetic field (above), caused by electric currents inside the liquid part of its core, stretches thousands of miles into space.

Q How are magnets made?

A An iron bar contains molecular magnets pointing in all directions. If the bar is placed inside a coil carrying an electric current, the molecular magnets line up with the coil's magnetic field. The bar has now become a magnet (right).

Power station

Transformer

Transmission tower

Q How do we get electricity?

A Electricity made at power stations (above) is distributed along cables at a very high voltage. The cables cross the countryside, strung between tall transmission towers. Electricity is distributed inside towns by underground cables. Before it can be used, its voltage must be reduced. The final voltage varies from country to country.

Q How do electric motors work?

A An electric motor is made of a coil of wire inside a magnet. The coil is free to turn. When an electric current flows through the coil, it magnetizes the coil. This magnetic field pushes against the magnetic field produced by the surrounding magnet and this makes the coil spin.

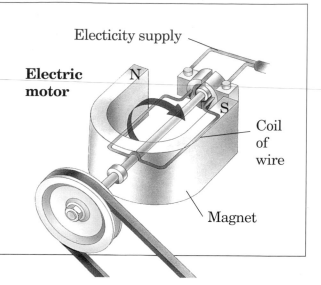

Electicity supply

Electric motor

N

S

Coil of wire

Magnet

Q How does a doorbell work?

A When the bell push button (below) is pressed, the coil becomes magnetized. The iron rod shoots out of the coil and strikes the short chime. When the push button is released, the rod swings back into the coil and hits the long chime.

Q What is inside a battery?

A Cars and trucks use a type of battery called a storage battery (below). It contains flat plates of lead and lead oxide dipped in sulfuric acid. When the battery is connected to a circuit, a chemical reaction between the plates and the acid makes an electric current flow around the circuit. A storage battery is recharged by passing an electric current through it.

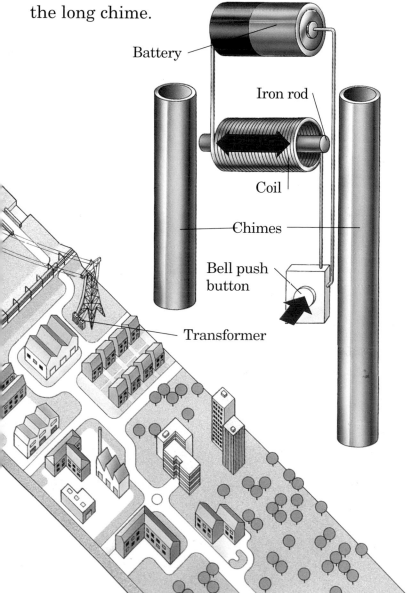

Battery

Iron rod

Coil

Chimes

Bell push button

Transformer

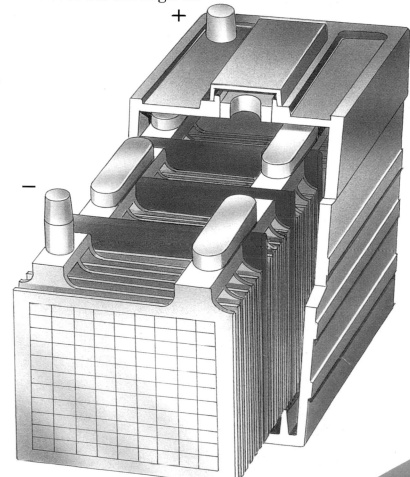

+

−

SCIENCE & TECHNOLOGY

HEAT & LIGHT

Q **What is light?**

A Light is a form of energy. It is composed of waves of electric and magnetic vibrations that our eyes can detect. The different colors (below) are produced by light waves of different lengths. We are unable to see waves shorter than blue light and longer than red.

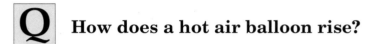

Ultraviolet   Visible light   Infrared

Q **How fast does light travel?**

A The speed of light is 186,000 mi/s, faster than anything else in the universe. Light takes roughly 8.5 minutes to travel from the Sun (below) to the Earth. Looking at distant objects allows us to look back in time. When we look at a remote galaxy, we see it as it was when the light left it.

Gas burner

Gas bottle

No.1 Staff Bureau

Q **How does a hot air balloon rise?**

A A gas burner supplied by gas from bottles in the balloon's basket (above) heats the air inside the balloon. As the air warms up, it expands. The thinner air inside the balloon is lighter than the surrounding air, so the balloon floats upwards.

Q **How does a laser work?**

A Light is normally composed of different wavelengths (colors) mixed at random. A laser produces an intense beam of high-energy light in which all the light is of the same wavelength. The process is started by an electric current or a flash of light from a flash tube which causes a gas or ruby rod (below) to send out the laser beam.

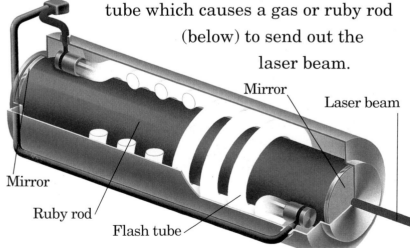

Mirror

Laser beam

Mirror

Ruby rod

Flash tube

Q **What are thermals?**

A Birds can often be seen gliding in tight circles, being carried upwards by rising columns of air called thermals (right). Ground heated by the Sun warms the air above it. The warm air rises, sucking cool air in below it. That, too, is warmed and rises up. Glider pilots use thermals. They circle and climb inside one thermal, then glide to the next (below).

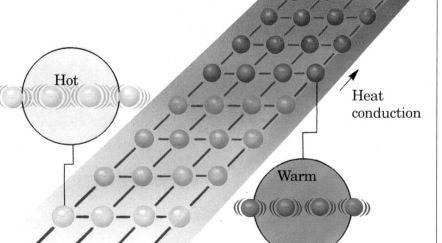

Bird's flight path

Thermal

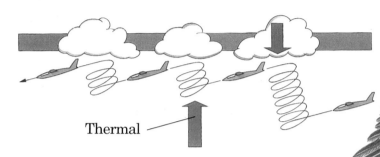

Thermal

Q **How does a fluorescent tube work?**

A A hot wire inside the tube sends out particles called electrons, which crash into atoms of mercury gas. The mercury atoms give out invisible ultraviolet radiation. The white phosphorus coating in the tube (below) changes this into bright visible light.

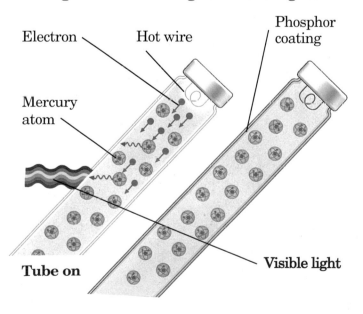

Electron   Hot wire   Phosphor coating

Mercury atom

Tube on

Visible light

Tube off

Q **How does heat move along a metal bar?**

A When something is heated, its atoms vibrate. If one end of a metal bar is heated, the atoms at that end vibrate more than the atoms at the cold end. The vibration spreads along the bar from atom to atom. The spread of heat in this way is called conduction. Metals are good conductors of heat.

Cold

Hot

Warm

Heat conduction

SCIENCE & TECHNOLOGY

SHIPS

Q What is the largest ship afloat?

A The world's largest ships are cargo vessels. The largest of these are the supertankers that carry oil around the world (left). The largest ship afloat today is the oil tanker *Jahre Viking*. It is 1,502 feet long and 226 feet across. Its cavernous hull extends 82 feet below the water-line. When it is fully loaded with crude oil, it weighs 621,500 tons.

Q How does a lifeboat work?

A When a distress message is received, a lifeboat is quickly on its way. It may be launched from a carriage, down a slipway, or from a permanent mooring which the crew reaches by small boat. Lifeboats are designed to operate in rough seas. Most can turn themselves the right way up if they capsize.

Q What is inside a submarine?

A A submarine (below) contains a pressurized compartment where the crew lives and works. The space between this and the outer hull contains a series of fuel, oil, water, waste and ballast tanks. When the ballast tanks are flooded with sea water, the submarine becomes heavier than the surrounding water and sinks. When air is pumped into the tanks, forcing the water out, the submarine becomes lighter and rises.

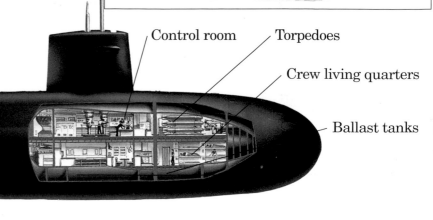

Control room   Torpedoes

Crew living quarters

Ballast tanks

Engine room

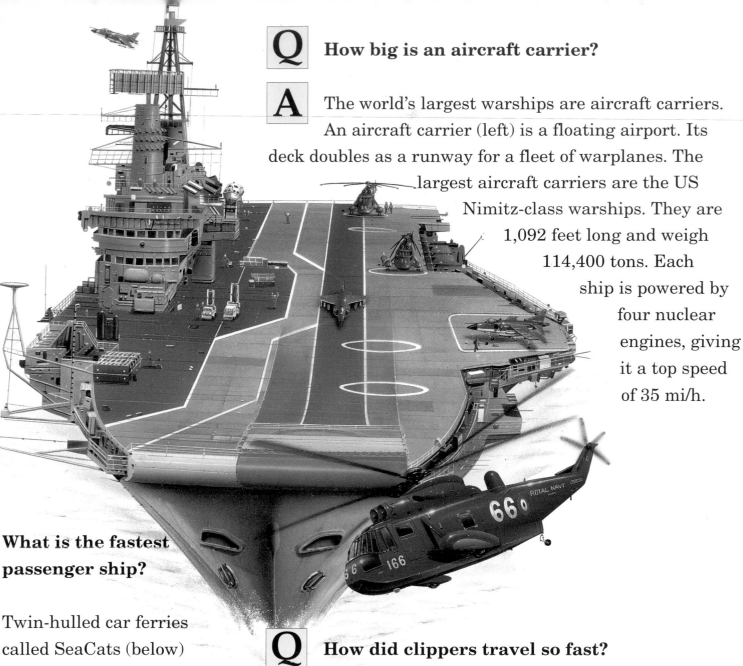

Q How big is an aircraft carrier?

A The world's largest warships are aircraft carriers. An aircraft carrier (left) is a floating airport. Its deck doubles as a runway for a fleet of warplanes. The largest aircraft carriers are the US Nimitz-class warships. They are 1,092 feet long and weigh 114,400 tons. Each ship is powered by four nuclear engines, giving it a top speed of 35 mi/h.

Q What is the fastest passenger ship?

A Twin-hulled car ferries called SeaCats (below) cruise at a speed of 40 mi/h. They can reach a top speed of 48 mi/h. SeaCats are powered by water-jet engines. Instead of propellers, they pump water backwards at great speed to propel the ship forwards.

Q How did clippers travel so fast?

A Clippers (below) were the fastest sailing ships of the 19th century. Their narrow hulls slipped through the water easily. They carried a large sail area to catch as much wind as possible. The fastest clippers, such as the *Cutty Sark*, carried almost 3,600 square yards of sail and could reach a speed of nearly 20 mi/h.

SCIENCE & TECHNOLOGY

Q How did early diving suits work?

A Early diving equipment made in the 1600s and 1700s worked by pumping air down a hose from the surface into a metal helmet over the diver's head (right). The pressure of the air inside the helmet stopped water from rising up inside.

Q How does a pressurized diving suit work?

A A pressurized diving suit (below) is supplied with air pumped from the surface through a hose. The diver can alter the air pressure inside the suit by adjusting a valve in the helmet. Heavy metal boots help to keep the diver weighted down on the seabed.

Q What is an atmospheric diving suit?

A An atmospheric diving suit (below) is a watertight suit of armor used for the deepest dives. The diver breathes air at atmospheric pressure, which is that of surface air. The heavy metal suit with watertight joints stops the huge water pressure 1,000 feet below the surface from crushing it.

Q What is an aqualung?

A An aqualung (above) is a device that enables divers to move around freely under water without any connection with the surface. The diver breathes air from tanks worn on the back.

Q How are shipwrecks explored?

A Sunken ships can tell us a lot about the sailors who sailed them and the world they lived in. The ship's timbers may be all that is left, but sometimes the divers who explore shipwrecks (right) find tools, guns and some of the sailors' belongings.

Q What animals have been found in the ocean depths?

A Light does not reach the bottom of the ocean. Many of the fish that live there make their own light. They catch smaller fish by dangling a glowing lure over their mouth. Smaller fish swim towards the lure and straight into the fish's mouth.

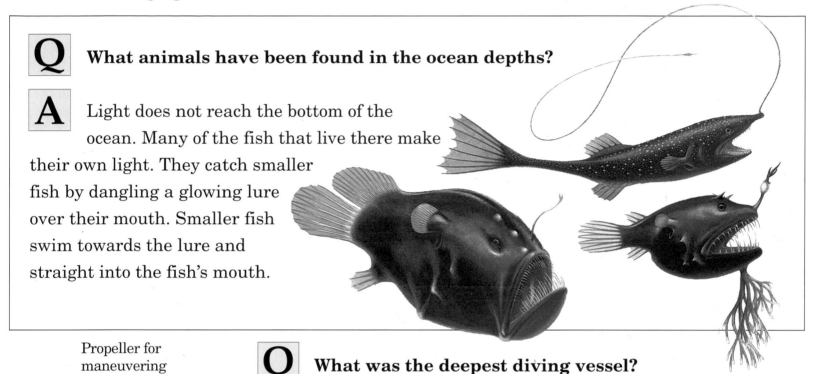

Q What was the deepest diving vessel?

A On January 23, 1960, the bathyscaphe *Trieste* (left) descended 35,804 feet into the deepest part of the Marianas Trench in the Pacific Ocean. No one has dived deeper. *Trieste*'s crew of two were protected inside a thick metal sphere beneath a large float partly filled with gasoline. When sea water flooded into the float, *Trieste* sank. To return to the surface, it dropped metal weights.

Propeller for maneuvering

Water ballast tank

Buoyancy tank

Crew compartment

Mechanical arm

TV camera

FLIGHT

Q How does an airplane stay in the air?

A Airplanes (left) can fly because of the shape of their wings. The top of the wing is more curved than the bottom. Air rushing over the top of the wings travels farther and faster than the air flowing underneath. This produces lower air pressure above the wings than below them (below), causing the wings to lift.

Airflow

Jet of hot air

Fan

Combustion chamber

Q How does a jet engine work?

A A large spinning fan at the front of the engine (above) sucks in air. The air is then compressed and heated by burning fuel in the combustion chamber. This makes the air expand quickly. A jet of hot air rushes out of the back of the engine and pushes the airplane forwards.

Q What happens before take-off?

A An airliner (below) is carefully prepared for each flight. The passenger cabin is cleaned. Meals and luggage are loaded. The fuel tanks are filled. Engineers check the plane and the crew make their preflight checks.

Q What did the first airplane look like?

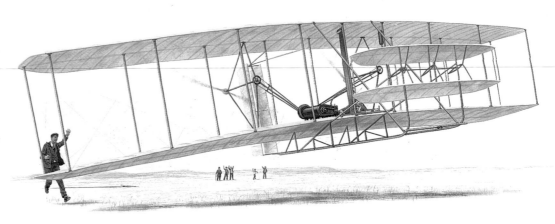

A The first airplane, called *Flyer 1* (right), flew in 1903. It was made from wood. It had two wings covered with fabric, one above the other, and the pilot lay down on the lower wing to fly it.

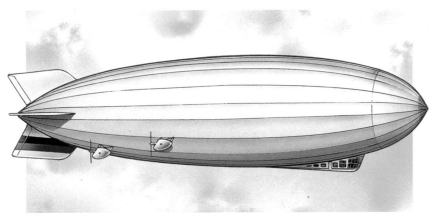

Q What is a Zeppelin?

A A Zeppelin (left) is a giant airship named after its inventor, Count Ferdinand von Zeppelin. The Zeppelins were built in Germany between 1900 and the 1930s. The biggest passenger-carrying Zeppelins were the *Graf Zeppelin* and the *Hindenberg*. They carried passengers across the Atlantic Ocean. Zeppelins could fly without wings because they were filled with hydrogen gas. This is lighter than air and made the airships float upward.

Hindenberg

Concorde

Q Which aircraft can carry the largest cargo?

A The Airbus Super Transporter A300-600ST Beluga has the largest cargo hold of any aircraft. It can carry up to 45 tons of cargo in a hold that is 120 feet long and up to 24 feet wide. Belugas are built from Airbus A300 airliners. They replace the Super Guppy transporter (below). The Super Guppies were built to transport parts of the giant Saturn 5 moon rockets.

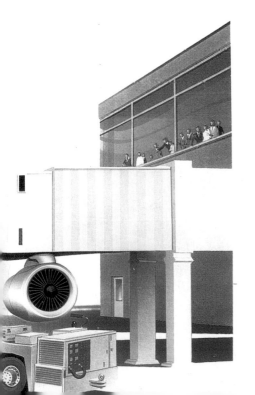

AIRBUS SKYLINK

F-BTGV

SCIENCE & TECHNOLOGY

Q How are heavy loads carried by road?

A The largest and heaviest loads are carried on a special low trailer pulled by a powerful tractor unit (right). This vehicle has six axles to spread the load. The tractor unit has six sets of wheels. Four of them are driven by the engine to give maximum power.

Tractor unit

Trailer

Q How does a refrigeration truck keep its cargo cold?

A Cargoes that have to be kept cold are transported in a refrigerated truck (below). The insulated trailer has a refrigeration unit on the front. Liquid coolant flows through pipes in the trailer and absorbs heat from the cargo. The coolant returns to the refrigeration unit and gives up its heat to the outside air. It is then compressed to turn it back into a cold liquid and recirculated through the trailer.

Refrigeration unit

Q Which were the largest ever steam trains?

A The largest steam locomotives ever built were five giants called Big Boys. They were built in the 1940s for the Union Pacific Railroad. The locomotive and its coal tender (right) were almost 130 feet long, 10 feet wide and 16 feet high. They weighed nearly 600 tons. They pulled up to 4,400 tons of freight in the Rocky Mountains.

Q Can the Sun power vehicles?

A Sunshine can be turned into electricity by solar cells. A vehicle covered with solar cells can produce enough electricity to drive an electric motor. A solar-powered bicycle crossed Australia at an average speed of 31 mi/h. The fastest solar-powered car, Sunraycer, was capable of a top speed of 48 mi/h.

Q What is the fastest train?

A The world's fastest train in service today is the French TGV (Train à Grande Vitesse) Atlantique. The first of these high-speed electric trains was introduced in 1981. On May 18, 1990, a TGV Atlantique train (right) reached the record-breaking speed of 319 mi/h between Courtalain and Tours. In everyday passenger service, TGV Atlantiques normally travel at up to 186 mi/h.

Q What is a supercar?

A Supercars are the super saloons and super sports models of the car world. They are fast, powerful and very expensive. The Ferrari F40 (right) is certainly a supercar. One of the world's fastest production cars, it can reach a top speed of 202 mi/h. One special feature is that the engine is behind the driver.

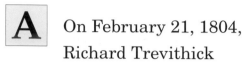

Q When was the first locomotive invented?

A On February 21, 1804, Richard Trevithick demonstrated his latest invention at the Penydarren mining railway in Wales. It was the world's first railway locomotive (right). It made a journey of 10 miles in four hours pulling 11 tons of iron on which 70 men sat.

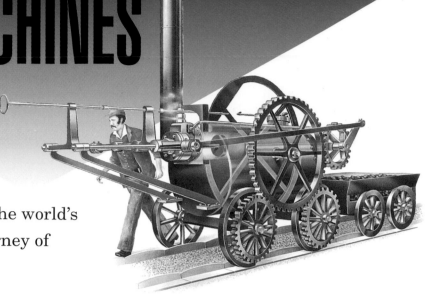

Q What is a bulldozer?

A A bulldozer is a machine used mainly on building sites to shift earth. It has caterpillar tracks to grip soft ground and a blade at the front that can be raised or lowered. To scrape the ground level, the bulldozer drives forwards with the blade lowered.

Q How does a hovercraft work?

A A hovercraft (below) travels over land and water by floating on top of a cushion of air. Powerful fans inside the hovercraft suck air down underneath it. A flexible rubber skirt around the edge of the hovercraft holds the air in as the craft rises. Propellers above the deck spin around to push the hovercraft forward.

Air   Fan

Propeller

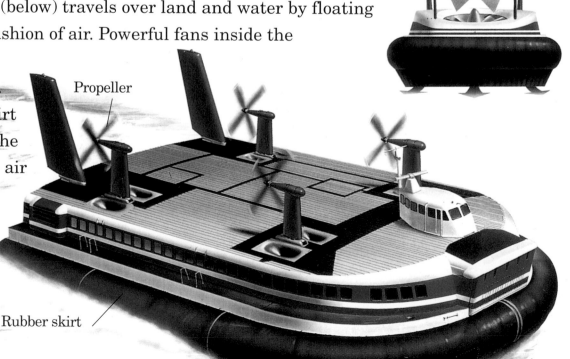

Rubber skirt

Jib

Driver in cab

Weight to balance load

Q **How does a tower crane work?**

A A tower crane (right) moves materials on a building site. A hook is suspended from a trolley that can move along the jib. The jib can swing around. The hook is raised by a motor which winds a cable around a drum. The open frame of the tower and jib saves weight.

Q **How do machines study the Earth?**

A Satellites orbiting the Earth are observing our planet all the time. Seasat (below) bounced radar signals off the sea to carry out oceanographic research. Other satellites measure the temperature of the sea and land, wind speed and direction, the height of waves, and pollution. They also measure forest clearance, iceberg movements, crop diseases, volcanic eruptions and the ocean floor.

Radar signals

Sea surface

Seabed

Q **How does a robot arm work?**

A Robot arms are used in industry for cutting, drilling, welding and painting. Their joints are driven by motors which are controlled by a computer. Different tools can be fitted to the arm's mechanical hand and then its computer can be programmed to make it carry out different jobs.

BUILDINGS

Q **Why was the Great Wall of China built?**

A The Great Wall of China (right) was built by Chinese emperors to keep out invaders. Most of it was built by the emperor Qin Shih Huang Ti between 221 BC and 204 BC. The wall finally reached a length of over 3,700 miles. Much of the wall is still standing today.

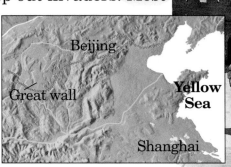

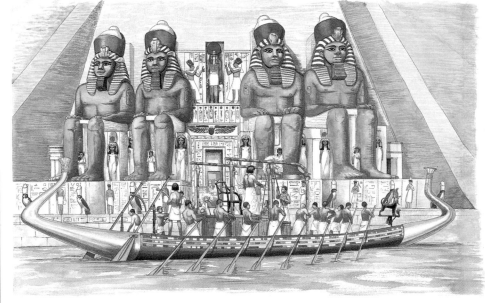

Q **What is Abu Simbel?**

A Abu Simbel is a place in Egypt where the Egyptian king, Rameses II, built two temples in about 1,250 BC. They were cut into blocks and rebuilt on higher ground in the 1960s when the rising waters of Lake Nasser threatened to cover them.

Q **Which building materials did the Romans use?**

A Most Roman buildings (right) were made from bricks and concrete. Stone and glass were more expensive, so they were only used for important buildings. Romans were experts at building arches. They built a temporary wooden arch first, then covered it with bricks and poured concrete over the top. Finally the wooden arch was removed.

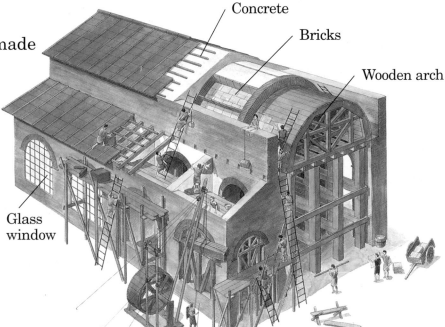

Concrete

Bricks

Wooden arch

Glass window

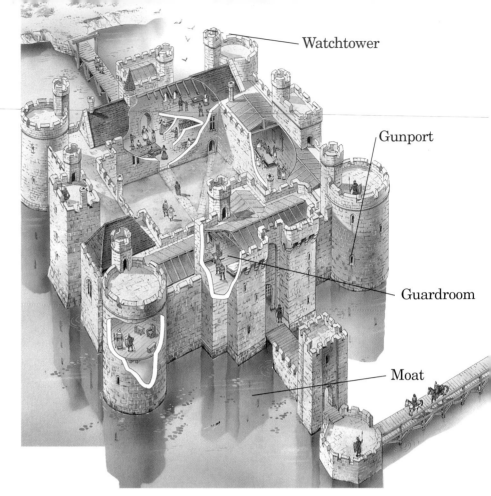

Watchtower

Gunport

Guardroom

Moat

Q Why were castles built?

A Castles were built to protect the people who lived in them. They were often built on hilltops or surrounded by water to make them easier to defend. Bodiam Castle (right) was a manor house in Sussex, England, that was strengthened to resist French attacks in the 1300s.

Q Why was the Statue of Liberty built?

A The Statue of Liberty (above) stands on an island at the entrance to New York harbor. It was a gift from France to the US in 1886 to celebrate the American Revolution. It is made from copper sheeting, and with its base stands 305 feet high. Its rusting iron skeleton was replaced by stainless steel in the 1980s.

Q What is a skyscraper?

A A skyscraper is a very tall building supported by a steel frame inside it. The world's most famous skyscraper is the Empire State Building in New York (right). Built in 1931, it stands 1,250 feet tall. The tallest skyscrapers today are the twin Petronas Towers in Malaysia. They stand 1,483 feet high, 499 feet taller than the Eiffel Tower in Paris, France, which was itself the tallest building in the world until 1930.

Eiffel Tower

Empire State Building

Petronas Towers

SCIENCE & TECHNOLOGY

Q How long did it take to build the Great Pyramid?

A The Great Pyramid was built as a tomb for King Khufu, also called Cheops. It is at Giza, in Egypt. Work began in about 2,575 BC. It took thousands of people about 25 years to assemble it (right) from 2.3 million blocks of stone. It weighs over 6.6 million tons and is today 453 feet high. The Great Pyramid was the tallest building in the world for 4,000 years.

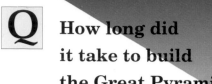

Entrance

Burial chamber

Q What type of bridge is the Sydney Harbour Bridge?

A The Sydney Harbour Bridge in Australia is a steel arch bridge spanning 1,650 feet. It is not the longest steel arch, but it is the widest. It carries two railway tracks, eight traffic lanes, a cycle track and a footpath. It was opened in 1932.

Q What is the Eiffel Tower?

A The Eiffel Tower (right) is one of the most famous French landmarks. Designed by the engineer Alexandre-Gustave Eiffel, it was built in 1889 to celebrate the 100th anniversary of the French Revolution. It stands 984 feet high, and is a slender pyramid made from 7,700 tons of iron girders.

SCIENCE & TECHNOLOGY

Q How is the space shuttle moved to its launch pad?

A The space shuttle (left) is prepared for launch inside a building at the Kennedy Space Center in Florida. It is moved to the launch pad 4 miles away by the world's largest crawler transporter. This giant is 131 feet long and nearly 3,000 tons. It travels on four double caterpillar tracks. The tracks are moved by electric motors driven by generators powered by diesel engines.

Q What is an oil platform?

A Oil platforms are offshore drilling rigs which stand on the seabed. The tallest is the Auger platform in the Gulf of Mexico. It stands in 2,860 feet of water. The Gullfaks C platform (above) in the North Sea stands on concrete pillars and supports production equipment, loading derricks, and a helicopter pad.

Q How does a flood barrier work?

A The Thames Barrier (right) was opened in 1984 to protect London from flooding. It consists of eight gates each weighing 4,070 tons. They normally lie on the river bed. If there is any danger of flooding, the gates are rotated to raise them up against the flood water.

Gate raised

Gate lowered

SCIENCE & TECHNOLOGY

INDEX

A

Abu Simbel 74
acid rain 17
adaptation 17, 18, 19, 23, 30
Africa 20, 23
   wildlife 31, 32, 37, 40, 41,
      43, 46
air 58, 62, 69, 70, 72
Airbus Super Transporter 69
aircraft carrier 65
airplane 56, 68-9
airship 69
alga 48
America, North 11, 25, 45, 70,
   75
   wildlife 30, 35, 39
America, South 34
amphibian 34-5
ancestors 23
animal
   behavior 42-3
   farm 44-5
anteater 40
ant 30
ape 23
Apollo spacecraft 10
aqualung 66
Archimedes' Screw 56
Ariane V rocket 57
astronaut 10
astronomer 4, 7, 8-9
atmosphere 9, 10
atom 5, 11, 52, 53, 56, 63
Australia 21, 46, 71, 76
   wildlife 29, 30, 34, 36, 41

B

bat 59
beak 36, 37
beluga whale 38
Big Bang 5
Big Boy locomotive 70

bird 36-7, 43, 63
boat-building 55
bones, fossil 23, 27
bridge 76
building 15, 74-5
bulb (plant) 51
bulldozer 72
butterflies and moths 31
butterfly fish 29, 33

C

camouflage 17, 19, 33, 35
canary 46
cargo 64, 69, 70
car 60, 71
castle 75
cat 46, 47
caterpillar track 72, 77
cattle breeds 44, 45
chameleon 35
chemical reaction 52, 53, 61
chemical 17, 52-3
   mineral 14
   pollution 17
chicken-keeping 45
chimpanzee 42
China 20, 21, 74
chlorophyll 50
climate 22, 25, 45
clipper ship 65
clouds 16
cockatoo 36
cold cargo 70
colonies of insects 30
color 43, 51
   brightness 31, 33
   camouflage 17, 19, 33, 35
   changing (reptiles) 35
   in pets 46-7
   light waves 62
   of races 21
comet 8
composite materials 55
compound, chemical 52, 53

compression 58, 68, 70
conduction of heat 63
conifer 49
conservation
   of energy 17
   rare species 18, 38, 40
constellation 4
continent 13, 20
coral 29, 32
cosmonaut 11
costume, national 21
countries 20-1
crab 29
crane (bird) 25
crane (tower) 73
crude oil 55, 64
crystal 15, 53
cuckoo 43
Cutty Sark ship 65

D

decibel 59
deep-sea diving 66-7
deforestation 17
detergent 52
diesel 55, 77
dinosaur 22, 26-7
diving suit 66
diving vessel 67
dog breeds 46, 47
dolphin 38
doorbell 61
drilling rig 77
dyes from plants 54

E

eagle 37
ear 58, 59
Earth 6, 9, 12-13, 62
   deforestation 17
   and gravity 56
   and magnetism 35, 60
   and moon 4, 7, 10
   population 20

   study by satellite 73
eclipse of the sun 4
Egypt, Ancient 15, 74, 76
Eiffel Tower 75, 76
electric car 60
electric motor 60, 61, 71, 77
electricity 10, 57, 60-1, 62
   solar power 9, 71
   telephone sound 59
electron 63
ellipse 6
Empire State Building 75
endangered species 18, 38,
   40
energy 5, 11, 17, 48, 49, 50
   conservation 17
   heat and light 5, 62-3
   nuclear 56
   sound 58-9
   water and wind 57
environment 16-17, 19
erosion 16
evaporation 16
Everest, Mount 13
evolution 22-3
extinction 18, 22, 38
eyesight 32, 42, 62

F

farm animal 44-5
feather 36, 37
Ferrari F40 car 71
ferry 65
festival 21
fiberglass 55
fire extinguisher 52
fish 29, 32-3
   in deep ocean 67
   prehistoric 24
   senses of 32
fission 56
fittest, survival of the 22
flags of nations 20
flatfish 33